>   " 'Tis time
> New hopes should animate the world, new light
> Should dawn from new revealings to a race
>   Weighed down so long."
>
> PARACELSUS.

CHRIST IN YOU

(Anonymous)

DEVORSS *Publications*

Christ In You

ISBN: 0-87516-506-0
Originally Published, 1910
Nineteenth Printing, 2002

DeVorss & Company, Publisher
P.O. Box 550
Marina del Rey, CA 90294-0550
www.devorss.com

Printed in the United States of America

CONTENTS

PART I.—CHRIST IN YOU

CONTENTS

PART II.—MIND AND SOUL: THEIR RELATION TO THE BODY

PART III.—DIVINE HUMANITY

"Unto you, O men, I call; and my voice is to the sons of men."—PROV. viii. 4.

"Blessed are your eyes, for they see; and your ears, for they hear. For verily, I say unto you, that many prophets and righteous men have desired to see the things which ye see, and have not seen them; and to hear the things which ye hear, and have not heard them."—MATT. xiii. 16-17.

PART I

CHRIST IN YOU

FIRST LESSON

A VOICE FROM THE HEIGHTS

I AM obliged to use your words and modes of expression, but I must say at the beginning that they[1] are wholly inadequate to convey spiritual truths. I long to help people who seem to be in the same mistaken conditions in which I once was, for man does not know himself.

We will consider together something of the truth of being, the most essential and the first of all things. You are not the outward and visible form; this is the feeblest and the most distant likeness of your real self. I will explain by illustration.

When an artist paints a picture, he does not put on canvas the reality; he gives you simply a copy of that which is within himself. The real picture is on the spiritual plane and exists there much

[1] I Cor. ii. 9, 10, 14.

more truly than on the canvas; the real picture remains for ever, the canvas does not. No poet can give you his true poem. He does his best to convey something of its beauty, something of its life, but even then it is far removed from his ideal. That, too, is on the plane of reality.

There is a vast amount of creative energy working in and through the material plane. Like the picture and the poem, this energy is invisible to you. We want you to distinguish between reality and shadow. The physical plane, or plane of the senses, is a shadow, a faint imitation of the spiritual and the only real. Your work is to show forth higher laws, to live and breathe entirely from the plane of spirit, to create anew from the very centre of all life, to make one the kingdom of earth and the kingdom of heaven. You are not to think of yourself and the universe now visible to you as real. It is this that constitutes the difference between us. *We* have entered into a larger consciousness of God, whereas *you* are content with the shadows of things. Just think how all your finest thought seems to vanish with the passing of great minds from your midst, yet this is not the case, as you will discover when you awake to the knowledge of a life that ever progresses from the unreal to the true. When this consciousness permeates the whole human race, you will be lifted to a higher plane, for the growth is simply a larger consciousness.

Heaven is not a place, but a consciousness of God. God cannot be thought of as a personality, since God is all and in all. The Absolute is above and beyond the conception of finite mind, yet infinitely meek and lowly, filling all space. As you emerge into this all-pervading love, the true life becomes manifest and is always the answer to the deepest and highest aspirations of the soul. It is love fulfilling itself. Thank God for NOW. Learn first and thoroughly that you have been, and will be, for ever. Your present condition is an opportunity for spiritual advancement. Make the most and the best of your life NOW.

SECOND LESSON

FREEDOM BY UNDERSTANDING

IT is wonderful to realize that we are one great and unlimited whole. I could not understand this once. Your[1] Scriptures tell you that all things are open to the eyes of God. How slowly we learn that God and man are one. Do away with your limitations. Stand out free in the strong life of God. You are like children with your walls and partitions, your churches and chapels. We, too, wonder why we were so long learning the things that have since become quite clear to us. God is all life, seen and unseen. Millions on the material plane are in bondage, yet all the time the doors stand open. You will

[1]Jer. xvi. 17, xxxii. 19; Prov. v. 21, xv. 3; Heb. iv. 13.

long to tell them this when you come to us. We are permitted to come to you at some cost, only do believe what we say, and act upon it.

We want to help you to live your real life. Begin by obedience to the dictates of the spirit within yourself; it will lead you into truth. This is not easy, as man is always hedged about by a false personality, a Satan of the senses—this shadowy nothing must be cast behind us, for it is of the senses and would deceive humanity. It is sometimes like an angel of light, so much does falsity imitate reality; you can always distinguish it from the spirit, however, if you remember what I say. The[1] voice of Christ is fearless, all powerful, the voice of a conqueror; the voice of the shadow of good suggests limitation, sickness, death. Hold fast to the All-good, the only real.

We worship God through Jesus Christ. There is no other way,[2] and there never has been, except in name. One title for

[1] John xvi. 33; Rev. i. 18.   [2] John xiv. 6.

God is Father, and it is the best we know, but it becomes much more comprehensive as we grow in the knowledge of God. You[1] have the power of a great victory within you, and God is continually speaking. In Him we live and move and have our being.

Many who are working among the downtrodden and degraded ask: "How is this?" "And why?" We would tell them that every created being must work up and through every necessary phase, evolving from the lowest point of created life. Yet we know neither the day nor the hour when the Son of Man cometh. Often in the deepest darkness of experience, illumination arises, changing the whole aspect and environment. The soul at once recognises that only through this period of apparent degradation and ignorance can it evolve. Make the most and the best of every experience, you will thank God for them all. Do not weep with those who weep, but help them by a mighty

[1] Luke x. 19.

love, pure as a mother's, for in the love of a mother is the unselfishness of God.

Learn to become unselfed.

You are not an atom, you are the whole. Every true unselfish life lifts the race nearer the Godhead. We are finding channels everywhere, teaching all over the earth by secret ways. Above[1] all things, walk by the spirit of God; as you do this more and more you will become conscious of harmony in your surroundings. Keep your hearts full of love to God and to all men, and we will teach you much. If you do not understand what we say, wait; we will teach very simply; but we beg you to realise our teachings in your lives.

[1] Gal. v. 16.

THIRD LESSON

CHRIST THE LIFE

THE voice of spirit is far-reaching. It is the expression of omnipresence, and is both near and far. It knows nothing of space, but for the present we must deal with beginnings. Perhaps it would be as well to help you at your present stage of unfoldment. It is absolutely necessary that you should have times of quiet,[1] that you should come out from the business of life for a part of each day. If you were to wait in silence, holding the attitude of growth and steady development, thinking above all else of the kingdom of God—your condition should not be one of strain or of blank nothingness, avoid both these extremes— the result would be of the highest

[1] Matt. xiv. 23; Mark i. 35, vi. 31, 46.

value to yourself and to all around you.

Hold in your heart, the true place of understanding, a stillness which is alive, like the heart of a rose. The God powers within you would assert themselves; crooked things would become straight, rough places plain. All smallness and discord quietly but surely would drop away and have no longer any power. To spirit, stagnation is impossible. The creative energy is constant activity within. All outside energy is waste and hindrance. As you quietly[1] wait upon God, the breath of life renews each particle of the body by its silent, orderly activity.

We are not able to tell you of future events, but we can indicate their trend, for each individual makes the future by the thoughts and acts of the present. You are to-day the result of your past. You may be hopeful, as your present thought will be fully realised in the future day. Hold the positive attitude in all that you undertake for spiritual

[1] Job xxxiii. 4.

development, knowing that God never fails. This holds you above the sense plane, and you immediately function from the spiritual, substantial, and only real. All must be finished before the Christhood of the race is complete—complete, unselfish, impersonal. Loving God and loving man, all may enter into unity. The evolution of spirit through the material is the work of creation. It is God that worketh in you now. Rejoice that you have this knowledge, and give the utmost for the highest. Live in spirit, breathe and walk in the innermost heart of yourself.

I want you to give some part of the day to this silent growth, thus bringing poise and balance into your whole being. I repeat this, as it is so necessary, so pregnant with results. First, you will be conscious of good sound judgment, a better understanding of your neighbour, and clear insight. Afterwards, the result in your body will be realised, for in the silence the[1] heart of flesh will have

[1] Ps. xvi. 9, margin of R.V.; Ps. lxxiii. 26.

become one with the heart of spirit; and thus you bring about perfect circulation of the blood.

You can understand how highly important this is when I tell you that the brain is fed by the spirit; a finer element has become ruler over the grosser, and the spirit of the living God breathes through the outer body of flesh. I am making this clear in order to emphasise the necessity for quiet. Later, you will not need this, as you will command at all times and in all places, heeding neither environment nor discord.

Do not seek love—give it. This is nourishment. Will you give ear to this? Take what is your right from your Father. He who brought you to this very moment of your lives is speaking in your hearts. Awake,[1] thou that sleepest. Christ shall give thee light.

[1] Eph. v. 14.

FOURTH LESSON

PRAYER

PRAYER is to us the breathing of the breath of life. It is the strongest spiritual element in all worlds. I think we may now discuss the subject of prayer—as I see you have used this powerful weapon to some extent ignorantly. You say to someone in trouble: "I will pray for you," or you wish to help someone, say, in Australia. You know your wish is one with God's will, and you desire to bless with your whole being—but how do you send forth this God-energy? The prayer is often sent with the false idea of great separation, to a God afar off. It is never lost, but prayer of this kind enters into the vibrations most in accord with itself.

Although something is done in this way, the person you wanted to help is not helped to any great extent. Remember, Jesus spoke to the maid alone, when He entered the room, saying, "Talitha cumi," and you too must be definite, clear, positive. Enter[1] into your closet, the innermost of yourself, and there see the perfect will of God accomplished for your friend—this is simple faith—and never see or hear anything else. Restfully,[2] and without strain, see victory in the name of Christ Jesus.

Now I will tell you what takes place when you speak from the God-centre of your being. In the strength of your calm assurance, the false conditions entirely disappear. There[3] is neither darkness nor depth where God is not, and you bring the troubled spirit into touch with God instantly. We have seen this many times. You cannot estimate the value of true prayer. To

[1] Matt. vi. 6. [2] Mark xi. 24.
[3] Ex. xx. 21.

us it seems as if you were like children
set down in a great power house, not
knowing the importance of the switches
and electric forces around you, waiting
for knowledge, yet ofttimes blind and
deaf.

I use your language so that you may
understand, but words fail to express
spiritual realities. Your faith in God is
your life and power. With[1] true prayer
you shall ask what you will, and remember, nothing[2] is yours unless you take
and possess. We have never known true
prayer to fail. Do not cast your care
upon an outside God and wait for results.
God being within you, the answer is not
distant from the desire. The spirit
within is one with God and Christ; how
then can God be afar off? I have given
you this advice for those who have
special need, but I would have you pray
always: "Thy Kingdom come" in every
heart and life. For he who knows God
in his own heart and in farthest space is

[1] Matt. xxi. 22; John xvi. 24.
[2] Josh. xvi. 4, xviii. 3; 1 Kings xxii. 3; Obad. 17.

at one with all nations, north, south, east, and west. In your love and prayer include them all. Live in the thought of love toward all, and your life will become one unceasing prayer, a[1] constant going forth of God.

We would help to give you poise, that you may live always and only in the central life, dwelling on the plane of spirit, the only reality. Have done with shadow and illusion—enter into rest. Cease from time limitations. Remember our first lesson— You always are, and you always will be. Try to realise this now. Rest from all anxieties and live in the eternal. The blessing of God is with you always and for ever.

[1] Luke xviii. 1, xxi. 36; Rom. xii. 12; Eph. vi. 18; I Thess. v. 17.

FIFTH LESSON

THE TRUTH OF BEING

THERE is nothing in life you need fear. You[1] will become sure that you are safe at all times and in every place. This realisation will reveal to you how much you have understood of the truth of being. Nothing can affect your real individuality. We want these lessons to help you to enter into your own now.[2] It is wrong to hope and expect grace only at some future time.

Realise that spirit is omnipotent, omnipresent, omniscient. What is there to wait for? Let me state here—spirit cannot be less than the greatest. You have been trying to make statements from without. Let all your affirmations come from within, suggested only by the

[1] Ps. xci.   [2] 2 Cor. 2. iv.

18

inward voice. Let[1] every other sound and sense be silent before it. Let[2] this spiritual highest YOU take possession of your mortal body. The only things that have ever really helped you to a higher knowledge of God have come from within. you must be true and faithful to the Word that speaks. Thoughts are thc outbreathings of this Word, the first cause of all. We can only help you to help yourself. Remember all through these lessons that nothing helps from without unless it receives recognition from within. The[3] spirit is always revealing Christ, thc whole and complete Saviour in you, the[4] hope of glory or gloriousness. Your[5] entire will, thought, and brain are led by this holy, invisible guide into knowledge of all truth. The moments of healing and growth have been when all the unquiet voices of the senses were hushed and silenced, when all personalities had

[1] Ps. xxxvii. 7, margin of R.V.   [2] Rom. viii. 11.
[3] John xv. 26, xvi. 13–15; Gal. i. 12.
[4] Col. i. 27; Gal. iv. 19.   [5] 1 Thess. v. 23, 24.

ceased to touch you, when you had learned to be still. Then[1] God spoke in His Holy Temple. Oh, that you would rest from your false thinking and BE!

Your present phase is a training ground, and you can do there what would be out of place and difficult here—just as you would find it difficult to learn the lessons of childhood when you are adult. Many loved ones who dwelt with you in the flesh have entered into the larger sphere to watch and pray with you. Listen to Christ Jesus the divine Man, and you will understand that His words are for you and have new meanings. That[2] you may have life in all its fulness, that your bodies may be perfectly whole, that you may be safe from harm and accident, that the worst enemy may be conquered, even[3] death itself, before you reach the thin veil which divides us: all this and more will be revealed to you, for all the works[4] of God are "very good."

[1] Hab. ii. 20.
[3] Cor. xv. 25, 26.
[2] John x. 10.
[4] Gen. i. 31.

To-night when you rest, do not allow the senses to suggest weakness or weariness; instead, allow your spiritual atmosphere within and without to enfold and invigorate you, until you are conscious of spiritual conquest before you sleep. Your whole body will be renewed by this holy baptism, and your awakening in the morning will be a triumph and a joy. The effect of this is a sweet cleansing of mind and body. So[1] much is done during the hours of sleep and darkness. We pray that you may truly say: "Awake[2] or asleep, I am still with Thee." Cease from worry.

[1] Ps. cxxvii. 2, margin of R.V.; Ps. xvi. 7.
[2] Ps. cxxxix. 18.

SIXTH LESSON

GOD ALL IN ALL

ALREADY you are entering into a wider understanding. There are many who have gone on, yet in ignorance of much with which you are familiar. So far we have clearly stated the first fact—Who are we? Indestructible spiritual beings. The living knowledge of this alters your whole mental attitude towards sin, sickness, and death. Now we approach with reverence and humility our next consideration—Why am I?

The whole answer is contained in one sentence: You are, because God is; but as man is still blinded by false sense, I will endeavour to speak from your own standpoint. In the place where you are, there is a work of the highest importance to be done, and no one else can do your work. God has brought you to this time and place in order to carry out perfect laws. You may never be known to the world, but your work shall stand for ever. By your own indwelling spiritual forces you will spiritualise and make real the plane of shadow and confusion. Working from the same spiritual standpoint, there will be no separation between us and you. In reality, there is no division. Your world sense of fear is the only barrier between us. This is a falsity, and belongs to ignorance and chaos. You are just where you are for the doing of God's perfect work. Hold an attitude of receptivity of heart and mind.

All the good around you exists for ever, and can never change or be lost. It is spoiled to you, because your eyes have opened to good and bad. The good is the only real. The[1] kingdom of heaven is like unto leaven, working from the very heart of God

[1]Matt. xiii. 33.

the Creator. Your work the angels might envy, for in so far as you are true to your unlimited and spiritual nature, you are creative. We earnestly watch and pray for the coming of the Kingdom of Heaven upon earth. It will be the awakening from shadow to substance, from confusion to order, from weakness to power—but, above all else, to the wholeness or unity of life. Realise that your work is the highest, work that you have undertaken to do from the beginning. I would here recommend that you begin with your immediate circle, as the very next step must be the right one. See and know only the good in those nearest to you. Speak to them, recognising the highest Self. Your trust shall beget in them new hope. In every detail of your life know only the good, which in very truth is the only real. Do not be cast down by appearances, but rather maintain an attitude of steadfast hope towards all who seem at a low stage of development, seeing always the goal to which they also shall attain; as for yourself, work with everything that makes for good. Your reason for being on the earth now is to help on this very work. There are helpers all around you. God is love incarnate. Peace is in your hearts and lives now. Behold, I make all things new.

SEVENTH LESSON

GET UNDERSTANDING

THE more we know of God, the greater becomes our reverence and humility. The infinite and eternal Wisdom has such exquisite order for every created being; the very stones and rocks are marvels of His goodness. Even the dewdrop obeys a law and fulfils the eternal purpose. As you evolve,[1] you discern these higher laws and become in harmony with them. It is one of our most interesting studies to discover the wonderful and perfect laws of living on each plane. If you could see the great interior worlds, you would almost worship your fellow-beings. God has endowed you richly. You have made

[1]Prov. i. 2, 3, ii. 1-11, viii. 14, ix. 10, xvi. 22, xxviii. 5.

mistakes, because you have not known yourselves. The mighty eternal love is seeking expression everywhere.

You ask: "What is the most practical method of healing the body?" Our great teacher Jesus Christ always met the need of the people at their exact degree of unfoldment. Thus, some would need the clay,[1] or bathing; others the spoken[2] word only. Jesus never failed to help in whatsoever condition or circumstance; that they came to Him was enough. This is where so many of your healers fail: either because they offer something beyond their power to realise, or because they employ methods that have become as words devoid of life. The[3] great Healer, by reason of the greatness of His love, could meet every need, and only as you love can you really help. Love[4] perceives as never man sees, suggesting with infinite variety the exact method. We are anxious that you

[1] John ix. 7. [2] Matt. viii. 8, ix. 20–22.
[3] Matt. viii. 16; Luke iv, 18, 19.
[4] John xiii. 34.

should not spoil the great and beautiful work by following any known method, but always by following your own loving spiritual instinct, taking "no thought what ye shall say. It[1] shall be given you in that hour." Love[2] with all your heart, soul, mind, and strength, and nothing is impossible to you. Jesus never failed to understand and recognise the perfect spiritual body in all men. Your body is perfect in spirit (substance), and every part of the material body should act in obedience to the spiritual, the only real.

When the sense would indicate pain and disorder, remember your spiritual body, and call it into manifestation by the word[3] of power. The[4] body should manifest wholeness, or you are surely making God seem a failure. Later on, when your body functions only from the plane of spirit, its uses will be finer, its obedience immediate.

[1] Matt. x. 19. [2] I Cor. xiii.
[3] Luke i. 37 R.V., iv. 32 A.V.
[4] Rom. viii. II, 19 R.V.; Eph. i. 19, 20, 23 R.V.

The positive spiritual man will assert himself, refusing to recognise the suggestion of the sense man, and will become ruler. Christ shall reign in you, and[1] Satan will be under His feet. Fill the house every day with strong, positive health vibrations, lifting the very atmosphere into purity and truth. Growth into good is so simple, so natural, for God[2] is working in your midst and cannot fail.

[1] Rom. xvi. 20.   [2] Ps. lxxiv. 12.

EIGHTH LESSON

FROM GLORY TO GLORY

WE are taking the first cause and tracing its relationship to our present understanding. You have learned to say, "I am spirit," "I am to create." It would be as well to understand at what period of creation the race now stands, as this will make our immediate work clear to us. The race is at present in its childhood, just emerging into knowledge of the great and only life, the I Am, knowing very little of its true meaning and purpose. You understand that in these lessons we cannot express spiritual verities in words, we can only attempt to suggest the transcendental reality behind the shadow. The finest earth-music you have ever heard can only suggest real music to

you; the highest that it does is to lead you
to the heart of the composer, where you
catch something of the perfect idea.

I have used this very crude illustration
to teach you something of the meaning
of God. He is ever beyond our highest
ideal. Here, then, is our call to growth.
Every stage of development reveals more
of God, and every generation of men
finds Him greater than the last. To-day
the conception is higher than it has
ever been, and yet you see and know
only[1] as men dimly groping in darkness and mist. God ever becomes more
lovely as vision clears; every height
we climb reveals fresh glory, and[2] calls
us to follow on with unabated eager-
ness. And yet His greatness is greatest
when it is in accord with the lowliest
atom, when the Father-Mother God
lifts the meanest thing to a place of
safety in the very heart of love. The
realisation of this fills us with worship
and adoration, for great[3] is our God
above all gods.

[1] I Cor. xiii. 12.　　[2] 2 Cor. iii. 18.　　[3] Ps. xcv. 3.

Jesus Christ revealed God according to your need. The world, like children crying in the night, and with no language but a cry, was answered by the Father; by this name you know and love Him; by this name we understand much more than you do; but God is always willing to help you according to your need. Present understanding reveals something of the law of endless progression, of the fulness of life, of its deeper, richer meanings. Jesus[1] revealed the Christ of God, the hidden spring, abundant, overflowing, perpetual, never ceasing, that you might have it[2] in all its fulness, that[3] your flesh also might rest in hope. There is no mystery in this. Full, rich, glorious life should fill every vein—for Christ[4] is your life. Jesus did not draw down life from an outside God. He knew Himself to be the eternal Christ of God.

I think you will see more meaning in the life of Jesus as you live from the

[1] John i. 18.   [2] John xvii. 13, 20th Century N.T.
[3] Ps. xvi. 9.   [4] Col. iii. 4.

innermost of yourself. Humanity, God's eternal son, will one day say: "It[1] is finished," and "they[2] shall all be one." God is everywhere fulfilling Himself; not[3] even a sparrow shall fall on the ground without your Father. As Jesus the Christ was unchanged by the experience called death, even so are we here, as there, ourselves, for we have always been and cannot die.

[1]John xiv. 30.   [2]John xvii. 21.   [3]Matt. x. 29.

NINTH LESSON

PERSONALITY

TRANSITION from the personal to the universal does not mean loss of identity, but rather a greater individuality. Personality as understood by man is full of limitations. If[1] the disciples were to keep Jesus of Nazareth, they would lose the Christ of God. Jesus[2] knew this and put the temptation of Peter far from him, as He knew His personality was not their greatest good. I[3] come to reveal the Father, and I[4] will come and abide with you for ever: these wonderful words were full of meaning and to-day come with greater power. Only as[5] Jesus withdrew Himself from

[1] John xvi. 5–7.　　　　[2] Matt. xvi. 21–23.
[3] John xiv. 7–11.　　　　[4] John xiv. 16.
[5] John xvi. 7.

34

their midst, could He come again to all men in His omnipotence.

I have shown you in our previous lessons that spirit is our first and real foundation. It has many channels and modes of expression, but it is the one and only life. Man on the plane of sense has tried to explain with finite mind the infinite wisdom of God. Man has limited the holy one, has dared to speak of God as person. Man, who does not know himself, has tried to explain the whole of God. In all these things you must live, think, and speak only from the spirit, for[1] the spirit searcheth all things. As you sink deep within yourself, a great meekness fills all your thoughts. You learn of Him who was and is greatest in His meekness and highest in His lowliness. The true understanding of personality becomes clearer to you as you realise your relationship to the whole. Your vision clears, you become filled with holy reverence and mighty hope.

[1] 1 Cor. ii. 10.

Personality is greater than you know, for the weakest person has the whole universe to draw upon—is entirely unlimited.

I say you exist because God is, and all[1] He has is yours. People seem to fail for want of vitality. The explanation is this: each of you is a trinity, living on three planes—the planes of spirit, soul, and body. In most cases there has been an unequal existence on one or more of these planes. You should draw all from the spiritual first, thus feeding the[2] soul covering, and manifestation in the body must follow. Only on earth can man do this great and perfect work. Every spiritual truth brought into manifestation is creative, and all your future is made by your conquests now. You must consecrate your whole being afresh to God, that He[3] may work His perfect will, bringing harmonious conditions into your life.

[1]Luke xv. 31.   [2]Dan. vii. 15, margin.
[3]Phil. ii. 13.

TENTH LESSON

THE BOOK

A T this point we will consider together the value of your Scriptures, the collection of books called by you "The Bible."

Books, words, letters, are all valueless in themselves. What[1] you call inspiration is the true secret of their value. The spirit by its potency, its subtle vitality, can take any word from any language, on the plane of sense, and use it to convey meanings, to suggest thought, and often to pierce through a wall of sense impossible to the word of itself. Thus the word is only the vehicle or outer shell, hiding either the pearl of great price or a two-edged sword. The[2] Word of God is quick

[1] 2 Tim. iii. 16.   [2] Heb. iv. 12.

and powerful; it is also sweeter[1] than the honeycomb.

Inspiration, then, is the one spirit using for its channels many books and many methods; it is ever seeking avenues to pour out the abundant wealth and wisdom of God. Inspiration is possible to all men. That you can from the spiritual plane use sense, or empty words, so that they become vehicles of spiritual power, is a great and glorious truth. This, too, is genius, for God has spoken, and the ordinary language of time and sense is made eternal and spiritual.

In just this way, Jesus took the word "bread," and gave it a holy and spiritual meaning. When we pray: "Give[2] us this day our daily bread," we are using words of great and significant meaning —seeking the nourishment that shall sustain us in very deed. In all things we are to bring reality and truth where nothingness and limitation have made

[1] Ps. xix. 10, cxix. 103.
[2] Matt. vi. II; John v. 32–51.

chaos and darkness. Then we see the necessity for light: God's first spoken word at the Creation—LIGHT.[1]

Written words are not the only means of communication, for the spirit comes into our outer man with great illumination, and to explain this you have no words. I pray that this may be your experience in all its fulness. It is the first and highest expression of God. The illumined soul moves through all life, radiating light, the unconscious manifestation of divinity, a deep, inward peace, a real knowledge of men and of all things, a light which cannot be hid, for it is conveyed in every gesture, in every spoken word. Thus we understand an inspired or illumined soul. The real value, then, of the Bible is in the spiritual or inspired writer, who has opened your understanding to the things of God.

Added to this is another mighty factor —the place you have given the Bible. It holds the highest place amongst

[1] Gen. i. 3.

all your books, and it always will.
Millions of people have lifted it by their
belief in it. In this we recognise the
working of a law unknown to you. I
can best explain it as the law of transmutation. The working out is as follows:
You can lift everything into the highest
place, until it becomes transmuted
and purified, changing into very gold
the basest metal of earth. This is the
philosopher's stone, the transmutation
into heavenly values by our faith in
absolute truth.

I am putting this key into your hands,
that you too may begin even now to
turn every experience into an opportunity to lift it into the highest until
it becomes purified, transmuted; pure[1]
gold tried in the fire of God; and not
only this, but it returns to you a thousand-
fold, filled with richest meanings for all
time. This is what has happened with
your Bible. You have given it this place,
and your reward is that it will always
reveal the highest things to you because

[1] Rev. iii. 18.

of this very law. Take the Holy Book and read it much; seek[1] the spirit, not the letter, in this as in all other things.

We are very much in earnest about these things, and if you remember that this beneficent law is always operating you will understand the effect in your lives. You have the power to bring anyone whom you wish to help into this place of blessing. Every act of your life, every expression of your thoughts, should be lifted towards the very highest. There will come to you a realisation of a place of sinlessness within yourselves, a place of purity and perfection that nothing can touch or soil, for you have begun to BE, even as your Father who is in Heaven.

The Bible has become to you THE Book, but I would also have you know that God has inspired men and women with power to reveal, in our own time, even greater things, and ever fresh unfoldings from the heart of life.

[1] John vi. 63; 2 Cor. iii. 6.

Above all things, we want you to have the open vision[1] to-day, for greater things are coming, and God is doing wonders[2] among you. Rejoice in the new revelation, abounding in[3] hope. The new will reveal the old to you afresh. Have no doubts. Launch out[4] into the deeps of God, and fear not.

Eternity is NOW.

[1] I Sam. iii. I; Prov. xxix. 18.   [2] Josh. iii. 5.
[3] Rom. xv. 13.   [4] Luke v. 4.

ELEVENTH LESSON

SIN, SEPARATENESS

TRUTH is the eternal Word.

There is nothing new, for truth has had no beginning. As you unfold you have clearer vision and wider spheres of action. You cannot see new truth, that is impossible. Whenever you enter into the plane of spirit, prepare yourself by prayer and the consecration of your whole being to God. This is the only safeguard against false teachers. When there is a threefold cord it[1] is not easily broken. Three souls in perfect unity can do great things for the cause of God and of all men. Let the spirit within you be your only guide. It is for this reason only that we come, that you may

[1] Eccles. iv. 12.

know yourselves. Our words can only help as they enable you to do this. Our love for your world is very great. Do not lean on any outside help, however high, however good. You have already learned that is is impossible for the mind of man to affect Spirit in any way.

The work to be done in you is of far greater importance than learning from any teacher. Jesus could not do His works of healing while the mind was thinking. There must be silence when[1] God speaks. The Christ within you is the same yesterday,[2] to-day, and for ever. Wait in silence and repose, that Christ may speak, may write upon yourselves His thoughts, His purposes, His designs. Let this mind[3] be in you until not I, but[4] the Christ of God is your only reality. You have known this for many years, but let the old Word speak again, until you feel the thrill, the newness of life,

[1]Gen. xviii. I, xxiv. 63; Ps. xxxvii. 7, margin of R.V.; Ezek. iii. 22; Gal. i. 11–17.

[2]Heb. xiii. 8.   [3]Phil. ii. 5.

[4]Gal. ii. 20.

the upspringing[1] of the eternal Son of God.

That sin may be forgiven, there is needed a cleansing, a putting[2] off the old, so that the tender, new realisation of Christ may not be impeded by the opposite of good. Sin and evil must not be confused as they often are. Sin is that great falsity connected with our outer self of the senses, it belongs to separateness and chaos. It would dare to set up its king and make its kingdom in our midst; but the Christ, now consciously real to us, as an inward fact, is greater than we know, and shall put all things under[3] His feet. His very life in us is re-creating, making[4] new, or filling with Himself, bringing the soul into unity with God; thus, as of old, driving out of His Father's temple[5] the thieves and robbers by His own right of possession. There goes out from us a

[1] John iv. 14, vii. 38. Syriac V., "He that believeth into Me, out of his innermost being shall flow torrents of living waters."

[2] Col. iii. 9.   [3] I Cor. xv. 25.

[4] Rom. xii. 2.   [5] John ii. 15.

cry of need, a[1] great want, a reaching out to the author of our being. The infinite love is all-sufficient, and from that heart of love comes the healing of forgiveness, such greatness of love, that[2] all is blotted out; since One dwells within who has conquered sin and death.

Learn that sin forgiven is the end of that sin, but[3] not the end of its results —the root is killed and the river of[4] life flows on. The suffering and results caused by sin can[5] be turned into good. We on this side see something of the compensations of life. The ways of God are perfect,[6] and the soul that is conscious of the living Christ, lifted into unity with the Father, becomes one with the work of redemption, lifting the whole race.

Love is pressing through the very atmosphere round about us and you. Love requires readiness and[7] obedience,

[1] Ps. xlii. 1, 2.   [2] Ps. li. I; Col. ii. 14.
[3] Gal. vi. 7.   [4] Rev. xxii. 1, 2.
[5] Gen. l. 20.   [6] 2 Sam. xxii. 31.
[7] Isa. i. 19.

and we are called to do its bidding.
Are you willing to obey even[1] unto the
death of the cross? That cross is the
place of your sacrifice for all men. All
must go to Calvary, there to become
one with the Father. Greater love[2] hath
no man than this. Love is the atmosphere wherein all that is highest is
nourished and fed. Love dwells in every
human life, however degraded it may
seem to you. Love much, and[3] Christ
shall do His work through you, for He
loves your world, and will never cease
until it has become the kingdom[4] of
heaven.

[1] Phil. ii. 7, 8.   [2] John xv. 13.
[3] I John iv. 16–19.   [4] Matt. vi. 13.

TWELFTH LESSON

"HE THAT HATH SEEN ME HATH SEEN THE FATHER"

HEAVEN is not a place to which you go, it[1] is just where you are. You can enter heaven NOW. Good men and women from time to time have made this discovery, and henceforth "All[2] is well." They have ceased to hurry, for the journey is over. They are no longer pilgrims and strangers, but children in the Father's home. The first thing we understand when we awake is, that there has not been any journey, or passing over and through vast spaces. We are just where we always have been —at home, alive for[3] evermore. There is no separa-

[1] Luke xvii. 21. [2] 2 Kings iv. 26; Hab. iii. 17–19.
[3] Rev. i. 18.

48

tion from anyone we love, or from any good that is ours. To enter heaven is to become lifted into a larger consciousness of God, and in this consciousness we possess much more really all those whom we love. We are nearer to you, and we often talk together. There is no parting, but only greater unity. No belief in distance and space is possible on the spiritual plane. I can only remember it when I wish to understand your conditions. In the clearer light we can no longer hold the false idea of limitation. All is ours and all is yours. To[1] become spiritually-minded is life and peace. No suggestion of the carnal mind[2] can ever produce good.

Thank God for the secret stir of life on your earth, like the sap in the tree, sending forth life exultant into every part. A glorious liberty[3] is opening up before you. The captives are being set[4] free, old bonds are bursting, fetters of

[1]Rom. viii. 6.   [2]Gal. v. 19–21.
[3]Rom. viii. 21.   [4]Luke iv. 18.

ancient creeds are being snapped asunder.
Be not dismayed, the battle is[1] God's.
Do not hug your chains; let go. Yield
to the highest within you, and so become one with the great good, pour-
ing forth healing and blessing through
every waiting channel. The whole race
is being lifted on to a higher plane.
This work is going on in your very
midst. We are full of thanksgiving at
the thought that you may know the freedom of the children of God. Conscious
union with God is your whole salvation;
spirit, soul, and body. The knowledge
of God's oneness with man, with yourself, is the open door to freedom. Jesus
came to show you the way, for Christ
is the Way.

I see you have not understood me
about mind and thinking. This is a
very wide subject. I can give you only
the main points. The sense mentality,
that delicate medium for spiritual truth,
has shared in falsity—separateness—
when it should have been the perfect

[1] I Sam. xvii. 47.

channel for the one and only mind. Crammed by false thinking from the outer, it should have remained open to the divine inner and the only real, fed from the highest source, the real bread and[1] true blood, which is Christ. IT is the power to bring into subjection[2] all sense perceptions, all false minds, alive in every part of the body. Every atom of your body should be under control, lest the hand,[3] foot, or brain should gain supremacy, rule you, and bring about confusion.

The sense of separateness in every sense is your great enemy. We beg you to let the mind of[4] the Christ control. IT is wisdom, IT is love, and IT is unity. Let this mind hold you, control you—sweeping through the outer body of flesh as its lord and king; so that each breath shall rekindle and glow. Ay, even the very dry[5] bones shall reunite and breathe. So

[1] John vi. 53.   [2] 2 Cor. x. 5.
[3] I Cor. xii.   [4] Phil. ii. 5.
[5] Ezek. xxxvii.

shall you die to sin and the sense of separateness, but live unto[1] Christ. You will read and understand in your hearts.

[1]Rom. vii. II.

THIRTEENTH LESSON

CHRIST IN YOU

D O you ask for practical lessons on healing because you want immediate results? I will answer your question, in order that you may attain to the highest. You can appeal on the material plane, and seem to get help quickly; this is because you have been so long under the dominion of the senses. At first, when seeking health from the spiritual plane, you will seem to become worse; always regard this as a hopeful sign. It means the last fight with falsity and shadow. With each attack of the enemy remember that Christ is your life; until finally you die to live, putting off the old man and his dominion, to live anew and for ever, for you have conquered the last enemy

through the Lord Christ. God's work is
never uncertain or hurried. It is sure, and
is steadily working out good. "Therefore mine own arm brought salvation."[1]
"Therefore be steadfast,[2] unmovable,
always abounding," and although you
may seem to make but little headway,
you are really growing, even in the darkness of night.

The great master, Jesus, unfolded this
aspect in His parables[3] dealing with the
kingdom of heaven. The little brown
seed sown in the earth is unaware of the
sun, until it comes through the darkness
of matter, by its own inherent activity,
unfolding to receive consciously that
which has always been influencing its
growth in the darkness; and yet I say
that even the sun would have no power,
were it not for the central attraction
within the seed. Now we understand
something of the meaning of evil and
its friendly uses, that the dark earth is the
medium for growth; and I can best liken

[1]Isa. lix. 16.   [3]Matt. xii. 31.   [2]I Cor. xv. 58.

it to the creation of God, which is called evil, always pressing into activity the hidden force within the seed covering.

Without this friendly aid and left to itself, the seed, though perfect, would be non-productive.

The so-called evil has caused the seed to quicken, to bring forth by its very opposition.

Look into nature, for therein is the symbol of every creative process on the spiritual plane.

All that exists is first and for ever in the real world of spirit, of which yours is but the shadow and semblance. When the fulness of time comes, your world will be no longer shadow, but substance, for it will be the kingdom of the Christ, the new heavens[1] and the new earth, one united home. There shall be no parting, for there shall be neither separation nor death, since the former things are passed away, and man and God are one.

[1] Rev. xxi. I, 4.

FOURTEENTH LESSON

OUT OF DARKNESS—LIGHT

THE seed covering, as explained in our last lesson, contains the germ—the promise—of the fulness of the Godhead, just as the outer man contains the seed form of the spiritual man with all the possibilities of growth and expression. We would have you remember that while the inner and spiritual is always perfect, the outer covering is often out of harmony and has many imperfections, owing to long ages—as you count time—of ignorance and sense domination.

You are to learn that spirit is the rightful ruler, the true owner and king. Man has tried to alter conditions on the material plane, to seek help from without; this has hindered and often prevented the real work. Wherever spiritual forces have been brought to the material plane, the work is lasting, nay, eternal. An unconquered body is an unfinished life. All must be completed. He will perfect[1] that which concerneth Him.

As you grow in understanding of the realities, your vision of Christ will be clearer, and vision[2] is the beginning of attainment. We must first see, then become our vision. Hold the highest ideal, even Christ, and you will awake in His[3] likeness.

You may ask at this point, how we explain the perfect physique of the undeveloped races. The difference is that you have evolved, and although through ignorance you have not developed perfectly all round, yet it is a far higher thing to have come to a knowledge of your spiritual being, even at a loss to the material. The undeveloped man will awaken later, and he too must learn the I AM. The will to be

[1] Ps. cxxxviii. 8. [2] Hab. ii. 1-3.
[3] Ps. xvii. 15.

becomes a force to be reckoned with. He will suffer, for knowledge is born of suffering, until he attains to the consciousness of God. As you have struggled with the less real, so will he, and you will watch and pray with us, till all the kingdoms of the earth are as the kingdom of heaven, for all souls[1] are the inheritance of God. So much of your suffering is unnecessary and caused by opposing the will of God, but there is a quality of suffering that effects the highest good, that suffering which brings into activity the three great principles of spiritual growth—faith, hope, and love. The highest good is known by its opposite, and every experience can be used for ultimate good. Learn that the beauty of morning is known because of the darkness of night. Sorrow is ever making channels for joy.

[1]Ps. ii. 8; Dan. vii. 13, 14.

FIFTEENTH LESSON

JESUS CHRIST—THE RACE MAN

THE[1] heart is the place of understanding, or as we would rather say, the doorway of divine wisdom— "Blessed[2] are the pure in heart, for they shall see God." The heart,[3] and not the mind, knoweth the deep things of God. Our lesson can only be understood in your own heart. The true revelation must unfold from the divine heart of love, beating in unison with your own. So near is God.

There are many theories, many explanations given about the cross of Jesus. Trust the inward and spiritual guide in all these matters, and not the mind of man. We know that the

[1]Prov. x. 8.   [2]Matt. v. 8.
[3]Prov. ii. 2, 10, iv. 33, xxii. 17.

sacrifice on the cross has for your world
the deepest meaning. In that sublime
act Jesus the Christ symbolised God's
highest thought for you. You[1] cannot
now comprehend the greatness of it.
Bonds were burst, and your earth was
given its freedom. How much we have
misunderstood its meaning! Let us keep
reverent hearts and hushed voices before
a mystery of such high import. It has
a wide meaning, and only divine wisdom
can interpret its greatness and its love.
From our side we see something more
of its results.

The principalities[2] and powers can no
longer harm you against your own will.
Jesus descended into the lowest[3] hell that
He might set free the captives and cast
off all that makes for separation between
God and man. The cross was the lifting
up of humanity into divinity. Every
incident in connection therewith symbolises some great inner truth. In that
mysterious outflow of water from the

[1] Eph. iii. 16–21.　　　　　　[2] Eph. vi. 12.
[3] Pet. iii. 19.

side, your earth received its chrism—its holy anointing—its Christhood. We worship in lowly adoration when we remember the greatness of that work. We have much to learn about this, and you can never know the full meaning of sacrifice until you too enter into sinless and selfless Christhood.

Jesus Christ is your highest conception of God. He chose to stand for your world from the beginning as the eternal Christ of God. He alone knew all God's meaning for you. When visible in the flesh He was the God-Man,[1] a Man for all men, loving God and loving men, the universal Man. In Him all find relationship. He is of the great wholeness of life, the sap, the very tree and vine. He was truly the Son of God and Son of Man. The great unity of God and Man is revealed in the cross.

[1] Ezek. i.; I Cor. xv. 47; Acts xvii. 31; I Tim. ii. 5, R.V.

SIXTEENTH LESSON

TRUTH IS STEADFAST—IMMOVABLE

TO receive this teaching you must exclude the vibrations of inharmonious personalities; it is highly injurious to allow an invasion of magnetic currents. This causes exhaustion and want of vitality. Keep perfect[1] poise of spirit, never allowing any influence to enter the spiritual innermost, while sensitive and receptive. Try to help people to their own indwelling spiritual wealth, and do not imagine that it is the right thing to help them of yourself. It is far higher to help others to help themselves, leading them to the true source of all good. I suggest that you do not allow any but yourself to open the door of communication between yourself and us.

[1] Isa. xxvi. 3; Ps. cxii. 7.

You all need to remember your own right[1] to rule in every condition and circumstance.

Let us consider together the meaning of the personal and of the universal, for there is much confusion of thought in your midst about these things. Jesus was both a spiritual personal identity and the Christ of God. This is God's meaning for you—with Jesus the divine teacher for your guide. Jesus the Christ became one with God when one with man. Only by withdrawing Himself from their midst as a personality could He really come again to His disciples in that interior sense which was to make of these ordinary men the great apostles of the Christian Church. Only by entering into the universal could He become the true individual in them and in us all, the You, the I Am of our life and theirs.

In that wonderful chapter of the Acts[2] you may find the record of their first glimpse of the great cosmic consciousness, the inner illumination which will cover the whole earth as the waters cover the sea. They emerged from the limitations of time and sense into a larger spiritual freedom. Their loss of the personality of Jesus was their great gain of the Christ all in all. You are to become one with all men, a great brotherhood and divine unity.[1] The words will surely reveal the truth. At present this consciousness is dawning; surely we see the coming unity of man with man in God.

You will in no sense be less yourself, but you will be greater in love and understanding. The suffering of some is the hurt of the whole. How[2] beautiful are the feet of those who carry the tidings of peace and goodwill toward all men! Silently working in the heart of the nations is the Prince[3] of Peace. We pray for open doors that the great interior life may flow out and expand, the very river from the Ancient[4] of

[1] Ps. cxxxiii.; John xiii. 34. [2] Isa. lii. 7.
[3] Isa. ix. 6, 7. [4] Dan. vii. 22.

Days. There[1] is perpetual healing wherever the river cometh.

Rest in hope. Be strong[2] and of good courage, the day is coming[3]—the night is past. In[4] the darkest and outermost hell is God. There are planes below yours, some even unconscious of God, but all shall be redeemed. Every time you make a conquest on the material plane, you make better conditions for those below you. I repeat, every individual conquest is a victory for the whole race.

Pray often and love much; do not falter on the upward path, for when you fall, others fall with you. Thank God for your glorious opportunity here and now.

Read[5] the Sermon on the Mount continually, and wait silently as the words unfold their meaning to you.

[1]Ezek. xlvii. 9, 12.   [2]Deut. xxxi. 6; Josh. i. 7.
[3]Rom. xiii. 12.   [4]Ps. cxxxix. 8, lxxxvi. 13.
[5]Matt. v. vi. and vii.

SEVENTEENTH LESSON

IMAGINATION

THE body is the covering and the garment of spirit, and you are learning that spirit is ruler. At first you may not see results, but the work begins the instant you function from the spiritual plane. Do not be discouraged—as I was—at not seeing results. I see now that the work of healing was going on, even when things seemed at their worst. You will thank God for the darkness and the struggle; you will prove their real friendliness. Christ's work in you is to proclaim liberty to captive souls, the opening of prison doors to them that are bound. Your body will be the beautiful garment of spirit, for salvation is not in part, but wholly.

You ask "What is thought?" Perhaps you have missed the true understanding. Thought is a creative process behind all phenomena. It is not a mental concept, though it finds its avenue through the mentality. The thought is never separated from the thinker. The worlds with all their myriad forms in nature are thoughts expressed by the Absolute. You are God's thought, and so you also manifest love.

At the very heart of life, both universal and individual, is the well-spring of growth, from which all true life evolves. It is the only ONE, the first cause of all, never outside Its own creation, but self-existent, inseparable from Itself; ever making for perfection and peace. This self of life is sending out rays of intelligence through its many channels, outpouring itself in infinite variety, but always One. The great outer enemy, the senses, would pervert, making separation even of the expressed Being, until, as a result of ages of ignorance, man has dared to think of himself as a complete and separate identity, looking on the suffering of humanity as something outside himself, looking on God as afar off.

God requires outflow from the great central life. This is a law steadily working itself out in the tiniest detail of your earth life. Your planet holds within it fire, water, and minerals of untold wealth, but it also holds a great invisible interior spiritual force, creative, reconstructive. This is thought, the outcome of the one life, breathing through stone, rock, and densest matter. Man limits himself by his mental process, and hinders the upspringing of the divine thought. (We see from our side.) Man gets a glimpse of a truth; he immediately begins to make it concise, gives it a form, clothes it by the mental process called reasoning; thus himself closing the avenue by separation from the whole. No truth is a part; there is but one truth. No man can hold all the truth. This is a work for all time.

You would do well to unfold the

capacities for receiving by[1] clearing the mind of limitations,[2] beliefs that have become bondage, and by becoming even[3] as a little child. Otherwise you cannot enter the kingdom. We see so much spiritual force imprisoned behind the closed mental doors of humanity. The spirit of God quickens the intellect, for it becomes enlightened by the true[4] light. Open out to this hidden spiritual life, as the flower is nourished into full bloom by its own hidden forces.

Consider well the flowers of the field; they do not toil[5] in order to blossom forth. You will become calm and steadfast, and the effect in the end will be a great peace[6] both in your body[7] and in your environment. It is God that worketh[8] in you to will and to do. Man's mentality is not the place of thought. While the holy seed is unfolding, the work of creation begins in you, as at the begin-

[1]Neh. iv. 10; I John iii. 3. [2]Matt. v. 21–48.
[3]Matt. xvii. 3. [4]John i. 9, viii. 12.
[5]Matt. vi. 28. [6]Ps. cxix. 165.
[7]Ps. xvi. 9, cxlvii. 14. [8]Phil. ii. 13.

ning of all things. God's thought was your planet. When the life upsprings within you, it requires a place of action to manifest.

That which you call imagination is the ground for the expression of God's thought. You will learn to keep the imagination pure and holy, free from the contamination of the senses; for that which is imagined, afterwards becomes.

Your Scriptures unfold the importance of this, when they describe false imaginings, and speak of imagining mischief.[1] A pure imagination is sometimes called "genius." It is the mirror of God. Let the Christ have full control of this, that you may awake in His likeness. It will reveal God's meaning to your understanding. Your imagination is God's best gift. The heart and the imagination are closely related— they act and re-act. The heart and the imagination should be pure.[2] This involves real effort, but you will be

[1] Ps. lxii. 3.   [2] Matt. v. 8.

richly rewarded. You will have the thoughts[1] of God, your mind will reflect them, and enriched and illuminated by the Eternal, you will be conscious of ever fresh unfoldment. You will see, hear, and know only God. This lesson will unfold within you while you read. God is the only reality for all time.

[1] Jer. xxix. II.

EIGHTEENTH LESSON

IDEA—THE EXPRESSED IMAGE

SUNDAY was a day of great joy to me. The seventh day has a deep meaning for your planet. There is a correspondence to your Sunday with us, for the seventh day is the Sabbath of the Lord our God. Real prayer is a great attraction to us; deep earnestness is the open door for its answer. It attracts by its magnetism, the fulness of its need. In our last lesson I told you that the place of creation in the individual, the spiritual ground for the projection of thought from the divine innermost, was the imagination.

Our next consideration is IDEA. First, the eternal mind; secondly, the thought; thirdly and lastly, the outcome of both is the idea, that which is to become manifest in the outermost plane of being.

What are your ideas for the most part? Are they only and entirely the outcome of divine[1] thought? Do you express the living Christ? I want to make clear to you the omnipotence of the divine man, and the reality of the God idea. Try and stand with me as you read this, and look out upon the earth plane. You will be filled with a longing desire to fulfill all[2] the law, even as Jesus did. The end is from the beginning—God, the end of all separation. The great Love will leave the ninety[3] and nine to bring in the remaining one, for all[4] shall be in the kingdom of our Lord Christ.

God's idea for your world and for you is perfection and nothing less. There are many who have passed from your earth still clinging to the false idea that matter is substance, the result of long ages of sense belief. Good spirits

[1] Isa. lv. 8, 9.   [2] Matt. v. 17.
[3] Luke xv. 4; Ezek. xxxiv. 11.
[4] Luke iii. 6.

often deeply reverent and noble, they still live on the material plane; it is to them real. They like to see their thoughts expressed on the material plane. This is a hindrance to them, all ignorance is, as they cannot unfold to the higher experiences.

Give[1] more time to quiet, that you may have the reflection of God upon the mirror[2] of your imagination, that you too may become God's idea, for He has said: "Be[3] ye holy." The growth of this perfect idea has become manifest to us. As you wait[4] upon God a great under-work is going on, and afterwards[5] it beareth fruit.

Close the door of your closet against the suggestion of the senses, that God's Idea may manifest in your body, for "if thine eye be single,[6] thy whole body shall be full of light." A full stream of rich life pulsates through the heart which is at one with God. This is the

[1]Ps. xlvi. 10.
[2]2 Cor. iii. 18.
[3]Lev. xi. 44.
[4]Ps. lxii. 5.
[5]Mark iv. 26–29.
[6]Luke xi. 34–36.

healing touch, no longer is the vital stream of the universe separate, it delights to pour itself out through its own God-given channels.

NINETEENTH LESSON

HEAVEN IS WITHIN YOU

MAY I help you in this chapter by giving you some little experience of my own. I think you know that the passing from the earth plane is different for almost every individual, and is entirely what each one makes it. The birth into real life should be exactly like an awakening on a beautiful morning when the dawn is stealing over the land, touching everything with a purity and freshness belonging only to the first hours of the day. It is meant that we should open our eyes and see God everywhere; just this simple, homely, all-familiar awakening into harmony and peace. God grant that you all may begin this experience where you are, then you will enter the more fully into reality, when that which is in part shall[1] be done away.

The consciousness of God is stealing over the earth, touching all things into purity and truth by its burning, glowing love. The fire descends and ascends, as revealed to you in the symbolic[2] sacrifice of Abel. All things are revealed to you in your Scriptures. Man has made this book the medium of interpretation wherein God reveals wisdom. If you only knew, you could read God in every inspired work, but[3] the Bible is your rich and hallowed treasure. In this ancient story you find the eternal truth of the two in One, the place of meeting—a place of sacrifice. Read carefully.

I passed into the plane of realities gently. My transition was entirely unexpected by my friends. For this I thank God, as my dear ones were spared the cruel anticipation and dread of separation. This was a great help to me, as I soon found I could comfort and

[1] Cor. xiii. 10. [2] Heb. xi. 4.
[3] Ps. cxix.

help them to something of my joy. This we can all do. What we cannot do is to rid you of false beliefs. This you must do for yourselves. You can never lose your own, here or here- after. More than that, you find that your own is greater, your circle wider, your loved ones infinitely more beautiful and even more familiar, for there is nothing strange in love.

Rejoice! Have no fear. Fear is the cloud that dims the spiritual vision. The[1] angels came to say "Fear not." Fear would keep you from all that is good. It is nothing more than an emanation from the material sense, and can be dis- pelled in an instant by the perfect[2] love. Man is rising out of the fear of evil, the fear of God, the fear of man. The truth will set you free[3] from all that separates man from God.

The very heathen are seeking God by the lowliest worship, for in their worship is aspiration. I discovered this when freed

[1] Matt. xxviii. 5.   [2] I John iv. 18.
[3] John viii. 32.

from the body. I was slow to comprehend that I had passed through the experience called death to find myself a living and breathing soul, never so much alive as then. It was too much for me. I felt overwhelmed by the reality and the unlimited sense of things slowly dawning upon me. Was it a delicious dream? You see, much of my false belief clung to me. I had expected a great, a tremendous change in personality. I[1] forgot that Jesus showed His hands and His feet; the same Jesus. How slow we are to believe;[2] but when we are ready to learn, we forget all error and ignorance and enter quickly into truth which is our own.

Bless and thank God for the knowledge of the wholeness and unity of the race. I tell you there is nothing lost into which God has breathed the breath of life. I thought also that I had not surely gone to Heaven, for I did not seem to be in any place. I had a new understanding, a fresh living consciousness of God. My eyes could see. The

[1] Luke xxiv. 40.   [2] Luke xxiv. 25.

scales[1] had fallen from my inner vision, and love seemed the very breath of being. It was too much to enter into. Then it was as though I slept. Oh! how can I tell of the awakening? Such an awakening will be yours too! The best and highest I had ever imagined was realised, the deepest longing of my nature satisfied, my purest thought answered. Spiritual truths were no longer in some far distance, but a part of my very self. This had always been; the only change that had come about was my unclouded consciousness of God. Now you see why I give you my personal experience, that you may know that Heaven[2] is indeed within.

It was as if I had just begun real life. I was a child with everything to learn, and from then till now the unfoldment has never ceased. Ever fresh visions, wider horizons, reaching after a richer satisfaction, to find that God is without beginning and without end. Love never rests in enjoyment of itself. Love must

[1] Acts. ix. 18.   [2] Luke xvii. 21.

pour itself out, and a longing came
to me to help those who were coming
along the road I had travelled. Oh! to
tell them something of the indwelling[1]
Christ. We love you all, and long to
show you what you possess. I want
you to understand that there is no
separation between us. We are interior
inhabitants, but there are other inter-
penetrating states of existence. Of them
I will not speak now.

It is a great joy to be able to reach
you with these thoughts. You need
not wait for Heaven. God—Heaven
—the whole of good is yours now.
Christ is God incarnate and dwells
within your heart, so near that the
feeblest whisper is heard, aye, before
you speak. He[2] hears and answers, for
He is behind all thought and speech.
He also fills all space.

[1] John xv. 4, 5; Gal. ii. 20; Eph. iii. 17; Col. i. 27.
[2] Isa. lxv. 24.

TWENTIETH LESSON

GROWTH REAL AND UNREAL

THERE is an atmosphere of rest and peace and much deep joy. An atmosphere of love is the one we can most easily enter. Everything is possible to the truly loving disciple. Love to God and man fulfills[1] every law. Love is[2] the key of all knowledge, wisdom and power. Dwell deep in this love, and you will see as God sees. Yet even this expression of God is imitated by the false or shadow self of the senses.

You will learn to discriminate between inflation, expansion, and real growth from the centre. Every good is closely imitated in the shadow world. Growth often means a great lack, a sense of poverty; it is never fulsomeness nor

[1] Rom. xiii. 10.   [2] I Cor. xiii.

aggressiveness. "The meek will He guide in judgment. The[1] meek will He teach." Learn the greatness of humility.[2] The little child[3] is all unconscious of its lowliness, its growth; so also must the soul be when really emerging; free from the unreal, the outer and false self of the senses.

"Love seeketh not her own." It should be nothing to you that others seem to manifest more of God. You and they may be at different stages of unfoldment. Be content to know that God is in the midst, and learn the secret of dwelling in friendly darkness, that your roots may go deep down; for during the time of hiddenness[4] a great work is going on. The soul that seeks nourishment from the true Self becomes strong. Learn from the parable of[5] the house built on the sand, and let nothing hinder this deep work of the soul. Know

[1] Ps. xxv. 9, cxlix. 4, margin of R.V.
[2] I Pet. v. 5; Col. iii. 12; Matt. v. 3, 5.
[3] Matt. xviii. 4.   [4] I Cor. iv. 5.
[5] Matt. vii. 26, 27.

that all is well, though no result is seen.

Seek the silence, love all men, bless all; thus do you make right conditions for growth. Unknown to you, there are outer conditions arranging themselves in harmony with the hidden work, and your whole future depends upon the true foundation being cleared of false building matter, wrong thinking and wrong actions, self-aggrandisement, not true material. There is no other foundation[1] than the Christ of God, the true self. That which is unreal must sooner or later be swept into nothingness. You are just where you are in order to do this work. Spirit is the only true substance, and our lessons will teach you how to build. God cannot fail if you are alive[2] to Christ within, and dead to all else. You may know the unreal by its self-seeking, by the desire for adulation, praise and self-glory.

"Be not deceived, God[3] is not mocked."

[1] I Cor. iii. II.　　　[2] Rom. vi. II.　　　[3] Gal. vi. 7.

TWENTY-FIRST LESSON

MATTER AND ITS RELATION TO SPIRIT

THERE is always a moment in life when we differentiate between the material and the spiritual. It happens in a variety of ways. Thomas[1] dropped the false belief immediately, when he saw the truth; material beliefs dropped entirely away and never ruled him afterwards. Pilate knew, when face to face with Christ, that he could never touch the[2] real life, although he delivered[3] Jesus over to the people. He had seen the eternal Christ when alone with Him. The whole of truth is beyond your present comprehension. No man can touch truth or stay the new vision now opening up to the eyes of men.

[1] John xx. 27, 28.
[2] Luke xxiii. 25.
[3] John xix. II.

One of the great hindrances to understanding is fast slipping away—the old belief in the solidity of matter. There is no such thing as solidity in or on the planet. The instant you ceased to be vibratory, your body would disintegrate and fly off the planet. Spirit is substance, and is not subservient to natural law. Perpetual motion is the key to the attraction of atoms. The whole planetary system is a vortex of convolutions, orderly and continuous. True, man's material body is formed of the dust of the earth, though with eternal wisdom and harmonious wholeness. Your body holds in its material form an infinitesimal atom or grain of every part of the globe. You cannot behold anything in that material world of which you are not a part. You are a part of the three kingdoms— mineral, vegetable, and animal. Thus man in the natural world has rule[1] over all. This is not so of any other earth-life, as each animal is distinctly and only an animal, but man in the process of the

[1] Gen. i. 26.

ages has come up through all, that he
may possess and have rule over all.

You are not matter. You cannot become
material, and you must not be deceived
by material appearances. Although the
value of matter in relation to your
spiritual evolution is very great, yet I
would have you know that spiritual laws
are supreme. Your body should be perfect,
for is it not a magnificent vehicle[1] for
the spiritual form? While in the flesh,
you learn to use spiritual weapons.
When you enter the interior and spiritual world, you will know that faith
was made real to you. While in the
flesh you should reach out for that
which is behind the visible. Faith, the[2]
strongest principle, is made your own
by your simple trust, though you knew
nothing of the reality.

Oh! the greatness of faith, the[3] power
and might of it! Have faith, for only by
it can you rise to spiritual heights, and
your earth experience is the best, nay, the

[1] I Cor. iii. 16, 17, vi. 19.
[2] Matt. xvii. 20: Mark xi. 23, 24.   [3] Heb. xi.

only means of revealing you to yourself.
Have faith in God, faith in man, faith
in all good. We on this side in very
truth have found that faith can remove
mountains. It is literally true that the
whole landscape before your eyes can be
obliterated by faith. This is a law; I
will explain. You see now only in part
that the things before you, houses,
churches, etc., are the outcome of man's
limited thought. He has been dimly
working out a spiritual idea. The spiritual
idea is the only fact, and not the bricks
and mortar. There is really only the
spiritual conception of a home, a church,
a road, and with the eye of faith you
could see the real only, for I assure
you again that the spiritual is the only
real.

In many instances the real is utterly
unlike the appearance. It is so much
more beautiful, for man is always working out the idea of God. Now you have
this understanding, you can sympathise
with an artist who says: "This building
or picture is only the faintest conception

of my idea." If he could only have the eye of faith he would see before him the complete spiritual thought expressed, and he would be overcome with gladness and delight. Thus at present you see through a glass darkly, ever reaching beyond the seen and the felt, that you may unfold the spiritual perception through mist and cloud, ever cheered by the hope of realisation. It is a wonderful time for you now. You are growing wings and preparing the spiritual body for its real existence.

Now, for your body I would have you use the eye of faith, that you may bring into operation the higher spiritual law. Your thought and idea become an outward manifestation. You become your own idea, but remember, it is you yourselves who open to the higher laws. It is for you to say, "Thy will be done in me"; it is no longer for the senses, but for Christ[1] in you, to will and to do. Creation is God manifest in the flesh. God is with you.

[1] Phil. ii. 13.

TWENTY-SECOND LESSON

"MY THOUGHTS ARE TOWARDS YOU"

I SUPPOSE if people only knew the true value of thought they would be amazed to find that every thought is as powerful as a deed, and in many cases far more effective than any word or weapon. Yes, it is your innermost and highest thought that makes you; always remembering that thought is the consciousness of the absolute will. You are judged by what you are, and not by what you seem to be. The judgment bar is the innermost of yourself. It is the judgment bar of God, and when our actions are tested there, the voice will cast into[1] outer darkness that which is not of itself.

[1] Matt. xxii. 13.

Thank God, you may enrich the kingdom of heaven, for many, many times the voice says, "Come,[1] ye blessed of my Father." Yea, truly our thoughts do enter Heaven. You will find your treasure[2] where your heart is—with God. In very truth a man's treasure is the continual outpouring of God's thought, and I tell you that God is enriched by your co-operation. Let His thought be your thought, and say in the spirit of prayer: "The Father and I are[3] one."

Do I seem to repeat platitudes? Read them again in your moments of sacred consecration, until the Christ within is the only voice, till all that is unreal and shadowy has passed away, even as the melted snow. I am glad to meet you on the spiritual plane. You need to thank God for this. In the very place where you are, if you could only see, you would find your own. I can voice your prayer—"Lord, that[4] I may receive my sight." You know the answer.

[1] Matt. xxv. 34.
[2] Matt. vi. 21.
[3] John x. 30.
[4] Mark x. 51.

Jesus Christ left every detail to you, and to the spiritually-minded I say: His words are spirit.[1] They are life. I would say to all: Pray without ceasing[2] the life prayer. Live in God in the smallest detail. Do not think the results you see are the only results; there is not one good word that is fruitless. Believe this and have courage. The very desire to help, if really unselfish and pure, is immediate help.

I have come along your path, and I would help you to know the golden, the priceless boon of right and holy living. Pause! Consider well the command until it comes from your own heart. "Be ye holy, for[3] I am holy." As you prayerfully express this, you will stand renewed, re-created, alive to the possibilities of God within. There are moments when we breathe the same air. You know them. Follow the spiritual understanding only. You now have victory over the less real, through the Christ of God.

[1] John vi. 63.   [2] I Thess. v. 17.   [3] Lev. xix. 2.

The human race is God's eternal Son. I want you to reach the highest bliss possible to you on earth, and in the flesh; that is, to hear the voice from Heaven say: "This is my beloved, in[1] whom I am well pleased."

Study the life of Jesus, and the veil will[2] be removed more and more, until the sublime sacrifice is revealed in all its greatness, the offering up of all to save all, and so to make the union of man with God complete. Do you not see the greatness of surrender? What you possess is of no value until it is given for the whole, for we are One in Him and not separate from the universal life; it is the basis or ground of all. You are maimed and hurt because of sin and suffering in your brother man, and again and again must the Son of Man be crucified until the great at-one-ment with God takes place.

Your work is to co-operate with God, existing only in and drawing only from the real, the spiritual, that you may be

[1]Luke iii. 22.   [2]2Cor. iii. 15, 16.

trees[1] of healing, that you may outbreathe God. Even as in the natural
body you breathe to live, so also you
must take deep breaths from the spiritual
centre, that your whole being may be
invigorated and revitalised. So much is
in your own hands.

I must remind you that regret or
sadness hinders the forgiveness of God.
God blots out[2] the sins of the past by
a fresh inflow of everlasting love. He
only asks for your need of Him that He
may fill[3] to overflowing with Himself.

Watch and pray.[4] Again—watch.

[1] Rev. xxii. 2.
[2] Ps. ciii. 3.
[3] Matt. v. 6.
[4] Matt. xxvi. 41.

TWENTY-THIRD LESSON

THE CENTRAL LIFE IS LOVE

I SEE you are theorising: never do this, but let the truth unfold gradually and without suggestion from outside. To make conclusions is to close the avenue and separate truth from itself. Nothing outside can ever help you or reveal anything until it finds its answer in yourself.

What is space? You are learning on the physical plane something of the rapidity of thought transference. Have you ever asked yourself what is between you and the mind you would influence? Positive thought knows nothing of distance.[1] It cannot be broken or interfered with. There is nothing that can touch its current, for there really

[1] John i. 48, iv. 52.

is no distance. The only necessity is the condition of receptivity. Simple good thought, sent out without any special direction, is caught up in the stream of good and helps all. Nothing is lost in the thought world. Space is a false and wrong idea, belonging to separation. Let your hearts and minds rest undisturbed in the thought of the omnipresence of God, until, even in the flesh, you may come to realise that there is no space or distance, for you dwell in[1] God and there is absolutely nothing outside God.

The sense mind would cloud or hide the vision, but NOW you are in "the secret place of[2] the most High." "The tabernacle of God is with[3] men." In all your afflictions[4] He is made to suffer. Even as the rivers flow out and refresh the earth, gaining fresh life and power as they do their work of purification, even so bring into the outer life the unseen and spiritual substance. Use every oppor-

[1] Acts. xvii. 28.   [2] Ps. xci. I.
[3] Rev. xxi. 3.   [4] Isa. liii. 9.

tunity to live that which you[1] know, and let your lives flow out and bless every brother and sister. We long to see your divisions swept away by the ocean of love welling up in human hearts and lives.

[1] Luke vi. 46.

TWENTY-FOURTH LESSON

OMNIPRESENCE

ALL you have ever prayed, longed, and hoped for exists. So mighty is good. You are laying up treasure[1] where there is no corruption, and all your good is your real wealth. You are making your future home, and your future self, by the way you live now. Rejoice that your names are written[2] in Heaven. We would fill you with more hope and joy. The souls that have perceived something of the illumination from the light of all men have been overwhelmed by the knowledge of the possibilities of their own lives.

Let us come very near in our understanding of omnipresence. God, who[3]

[1]Matt. vi. 19.
[2]Luke x. 20.   [3]Jer. xxiii. 24.

fills all space, knows nothing of past or future, but is eternally present. He is Alpha and[1] Omega, the same yesterday and for ever. The whole human race is meant to understand this. Let me explain.

You sometimes wonder at what seems loss of memory in us. We can recall anything of good that we wish. We learn the higher spiritual laws very quickly, and there is one that is best explained by the words "All time is the present." At once we cease to hurry, a great strain drops from us, all is ours, and we must take our own. To some who are here this blessed truth is a great part of their Heaven. When the eager souls, who imagine they must do a certain amount in a given space of time, discover this, the effect on them is to renew their energies, unfold wider prospects, and service becomes a rest. They truly begin to live. To the weary heart the present is enough. To live on the spiritual plane is to live

[1]Rev. xxi. 6.

in reality, not spasmodically and in limits.

Pause and think—How can time be divided? Day and night are explained to us as the inflow into and the outflow from the ocean of ever-present time. It is a wise law—the eternal present, the glorious NOW, a rest and a joy, a satisfaction too full to make us wish to look backward or forward, since we know that all is well. The sufficiency is the actual present. Think over this carefully, that your joy may be full. "I[1] AM" is the present tense for all time.

This beneficent and merciful consciousness is the outcome of love. Just think a moment what the effect of entering into this realisation would be on your earth. To draw the very next breath direct from God, with no past memory of wrongs or sins, filled only with the knowledge of the great love-life, assimilating all the good into the present, living the blessed NOW: think what it would mean. This is what Christ teaches you. To say,

[1]Ex. iii. 14.

"Lazarus, come[1] forth," was to speak from the spiritual plane, realising only the present life.

Do you not see here the true secret of eternal youth, each stage of unfoldment opening up a richer, riper youth? I am the Lord, I[2] change not. Open your eyes and see this wondrous truth. You can be just as much of God as you are prepared to manifest. Even now you hold within yourself the accumulated good of all the ages. Christ the Son of God in the heart of humanity reaches out to man until he awakes to divine consciousness.

The seven acts of Christ become actual to man, instead of belonging to a past period. He experiences the birth, the awakening in the Temple, the anointing, the temptation, the crucifixion, the resurrection, and the ascension. Christ[3] must be in you; nothing avails man from the outside, all is from within. Thank God for Jesus Christ,

[1] John xi. 43.   [2] Mal. iii. 6.
[3] Col. i. 27.

"the unspeakable gift"[1] of God. The evolution of one soul exalts the whole race. "That[2] they all may be one."

The understanding of time as a present fact would remove false ideas of inherited ill. In order to bring this higher law into action on the sense plane, the mind would at once cease to uphold the working out of ignorance and sin; yet at the same time it would not alter the effect of past cause, seeing that only the good that man does has any real vitality. The sense of physical law makes both good and evil seem of equal power. Good must overcome[3] evil by its own vitality. In truth, it is the real and the only real. Realise the present. As you read you will understand.

Peace to all.

[1] 2Cor. ix. 15.   [2] John xvii. 11.
[3] Dan. iv. 27: Rom. xii. 21.

TWENTY-FIFTH LESSON

OMNIPRESENCE (continued)

SO that you may the better understand ever-present time, I will make
this statement, which is absolute truth:
no time has passed since our last lesson,
it was and is NOW. Man and not God
made yesterday and will make to-morrow.
This is to you the seventh month in the
year 1907. It is the day on which Christ
was born, and it is the only day that has
ever been. Time cannot pass. There is
no past. Man is a new creation by the
power of the living Christ. You may not
understand at once, but you will. Can
you conceive of Christ aging? Have
you never discovered the wonderful fact
in the thought of the eternal youth of
the Christ? As Christ is, even so¹ are we,

¹I John iv. 17.

although it doth not yet appear[1] to physical or mortal sense.

You speak of us as the unreal. The truth is quite the reverse. We are on the only real plane, and your physical plane or plane of the senses is to us the unreal or the shadow. We find many vital laws exactly the opposite of those in operation on your plane. You are there to bring into manifestation spiritual laws, and Christ showed you this possibility. Water[2] was not able to engulf spirit when spirit was absolutely controlling the physical atoms. There shall no[3] evil or accident befall thee, nor any sickness come nigh thy tabernacle (or body). Your sicknesses, your disasters, are the result of your descent, or rather of your wrong plane of being. The Fall is a present and not a past fact. Man's real fall is that he is content with the shadow of good. He still eats of the tree of good and[4] evil, and until the Christ fills the whole consciousness, man will ever

[1] I John iii. 2.
[3] Ps. xci. 10.
[2] John vi. 19.
[4] Gen. iii.

be at war with himself, his brother, and his God.

Man's understanding is clearer, and light is breaking everywhere. You can read your Old Testament more intelligently, seeing in the symbols the inner and spiritual ideas of God. The waters of[1] Marah were bitter; this was the result of the bitterness of the people. Man makes the quality of the land; the flow of waters increases or decreases according to laws hidden within yourselves. You have made the very form of your island, England, by your thoughts and inner forces. Look to it that you obey the voice of spirit, for man was made to have dominion.[2] The very changes of climate, all seeming disasters, are in accord with the life and being of man, and until man has come into and unto God, back to Eden, you will seem to wait for the new Heaven and the new Earth, "for in that day they shall neither hurt nor destroy in all My Holy[3] Mount." I

[1] Ex. xv. 23.   [2] Gen. i. 26.   [3] Isa. xi. 9, lxv. 25.

have lifted the veil that you may see the need of giving the utmost for the highest. Blessed be God for Jesus Christ, the Son of Man and Son of God.

In the story of the bitterness of Marah is a hidden truth: ingratitude and murmuring brought bitterness. It is the same to-day. Your thoughts, if they are the suggestions of the senses, will still lead to bitterness and ashes. Learn the secret of praise and thanksgiving, the oil of[1] joy. Even in the wilderness experience the waters shall[2] be sweet. You shall partake of the milk and[3] honey. The[4] manna is at your very feet, enough for each day, for Christ is that heavenly[5] manna. Feed on Him in your heart by faith.

The very gifts you seek are poured out in rich abundance. Lift up your eyes and see. Just inasmuch as you yield to the divine innermost, as you live and bring forth the fruit of[6] the spirit,

[1] Isa. lxi. 3.   [2] Ex. xv. 25.
[3] Ex. iii. 8.   [4] Ex. xvi. 18.
[5] John vi. 51.   [6] Gal. v. 22.

to that extent shall you have access
to all that earth and heaven can yield.
There[1] is no want to the children of
God. There are times on the physical
plane when the way is hid,[2] and the
heavens seem as brass. You can open
the floodgates by steady thanksgiving[3]
and certain hope. If you only knew,
the closed doors are the senses, brought
up against a wall of their own construc-
tion, a wall of doubt, fear, and falsity.
A breath of the spirit of God consumes
them. You are greater than shadow,
sense, or clay. Having your feet on the
Rock, they cannot slide. God is with
you. Complete harmony will be realised,
for God is working out His divine
purpose in you.

[1] Ps. xxxiv. 10.   [2] Isa. xl. 27.
[3] Phil. iv. 6.

TWENTY-SIXTH LESSON

THE CONTROL OF SELF AND ENVIRONMENT

THE world around, or rather the visible world, is, as you know, full of wonderful possibilities, though yet imperfect, because unconquered; illusory and shadowy only because man has not reached the crown of being. As man evolves, the whole material plane is lifted into a higher condition. The seasons depend on God in man, and are according to the inner mind. The world is wild and lawless in some regions, so much so that man is subject to the nature or world spirit. Misused energy and uncontrolled force call for lord and master, as the trees of old asked for a king[1] to reign over them.

[1] Judg. ix. 8.

If you read this parable carefully, you will find much hidden truth. God made man to rule and to have all things subject to him. The world is gradually learning some of these higher mysteries. If you had a tree or plant under your control, in time it would respond, and assume its highest possible form, on condition you became at one with its hidden laws, and you are meant to become this. I merely give you this simple truth to lead you higher. The physical world is governed by its own forces and passions, and not by the spiritual, the only real. For the teaching of this very lesson Jesus stilled the[1] storm with the word "PEACE," since He had control over His own natural and physical self, and afterwards used the God-given right of dominion.[2] You are the channels through which the divine will and energy manifests its one self. To effect this you must become selfless and at one, for the Lord thy God is one Lord[3] and not many.

[1] Mark iv. 39.   [2] Gen. i. 26.   [3] Deut. vi. 4.

There are spiritual treasures hidden in your earth awaiting your appropriation. These wonders and glories are unrevealed to the physical or fallen man. Cain stands as the symbol for the spiritually blind; he speaks the truth when he says: "My[1] punishment is greater than I can bear." Christ your Redeemer is leading you back to your own. You are alive to the truth of being—the omnipotence of God in man.

You are now learning that the natural and sense body can have no control, but should manifest wholeness and love. There is a great and glorious work to be done on your planet: the Christ work of[2] healing—and this is possible to all who have spiritual control. We urge you to do your part. God never fails, and victory is yours. You will know exactly how to act as the need arises. Take no thought[3]—only in all things obey the spirit, and never for a moment allow the senses to suggest

[1] Gen. iv. 13.   [2] Matt. x. 8.
[3] Matt. x. 19.

failure, fear, or doubt. On all occasions speak to the senses the[1] word of power— "Get[2] thee behind me, Satan." God[3] waits to pour Himself out. I say you can prove Him. He never fails or makes a mistake. Do you not see what a beautiful work awaits you? You[4] receive by giving. The more you bless, the greater the power of blessing.

Love is the greatest of all healers, and finds its own way.

[1] Luke vii. 7.　　　　　[2] Matt. xvi. 23.
[3] Mal. iii. 10.　　　　　[4] Luke vi. 38.

TWENTY-SEVENTH LESSON

THE DEATH OF MORTAL MAN—
RENUNCIATION

OH, the inexpressible joy of vision! There is nothing higher or more satisfying. You shall know how to speak and heal in proportion as you live up to the highest within you.

Renunciation[1] implies a complete and deliberate stand for truth, abandoning all else. It is the step which, once taken, opens up before you the Christ existence. It is not, as supposed, the giving up of[2] wealth, position, and friends, to become poor and desolate; it is rather withdrawal from submission and obedience to the prince of[3] this world—

[1] Matt. x. 39. [2] Matt. xvi. 24.
[3] John xiv. 30.

112

the creation of mortal sense—that you may deliberately follow the Christ in[1] every thought, renouncing all other rights over you. Thus renunciation becomes acquisition. You lay down in order to[2] take up, but with a great difference.

Hitherto life has seemed a vast arena, where some are winners and some losers, where all who can fight may win, where the battle is to the strong. In this great game of life man gives all to win all, that he may become greater than all; for him there is nothing beyond. This plane is of the senses. It is the plane of death and finality. The forces of the sense plane control him, and that which has happened to him is worse than death. It is the loss of individuality.

The spiritual man has failed to develop in that form, and must seek another. Thus the mortal has not become immortalised, and is known no more. This is true, and we tell it in order

[1] 2 Cor. x. 5.   [2] John x. 18.

that you may understand the real meaning of the death of the sinner. The preservation of your individuality depends upon yourself—that you become the creation of God, a perfect man, a perfect woman, depends on your coming definitely to the place of renunciation,[1] which is for you the beginning of life. I[2] am come that you may have life, says Christ, and not death.

You possess nothing of the sense world. You are a spiritual being, sent out from God to do His work and will. The material plane is your place of action, and your work commences with the dawning consciousness of God. Your Scriptures are full of this teaching; Jesus has gone every step of the way for your guidance. There are pathfinders in your midst to-day. Follow ME,[3] says Christ, and the spiritual and real man renounces all, to follow the King.

How we love your earth! How we

long to lift you into true life, but the great and eternal law stands for ever. No man can walk along this path, till he has made the renunciation of his own will; by this choice man proves to man his right to divinity. To enter into truth, he renounces all that the world can give. You are on the spiritual plane to bring the kingdom of heaven into unity with the earth, that we may all be one. Thus you see how important it is to live every moment in the only real. We hope to teach you much; as you enter in, you must be full of that confidence which is the offspring of truth.

At present you are to conquer[1] the fleshly body, ruling in love, but always ruling. There is a beautiful work before you. Jesus said: "The Prince of this world cometh and hath nothing in ME." These were words of life and power. These may be your words too, so that nothing can touch you, hidden in God, doing His work and willing

[1]Rom. viii. II.

His will. You may reach the place where you no longer hear two voices, but one only—that of the living Christ.

PART II

MIND AND SOUL:

THEIR RELATION TO THE BODY

FIRST LESSON

"LET YOUR LIGHT SO SHINE"

WE have a glorious message for your plane, and our words are winged. They come with power and influence to all in need. You must have singleness[1] of heart, and the consecrated life, to be the pure channel which God desires. Is it not worth while to voice the highest and to bear the light? Our message is for the world of pain and suffering, and for you, too; wholeness and perfection[2] are God's intention. Our message will teach you how to attain. Every spiritual value must be desired,[3] must be lived. Our thought for you must become embodied, lived, manifested, expressed, to all men. The

[1]Matt. v. 8.   [2]Matt. v. 48.
[3]John xiii. 17.

two conditions we ask, that we may teach you, are that you become willing and obedient. Your life shall help all you meet, cannot fail to do so, because you cannot grow without drawing others with you. This is God's perfect plan for the redemption of the whole.

The seed dies[1] in order to live, and becomes hidden, that it may manifest from within. Out of darkness—light. Out of weakness—strength.

There is a wave of disturbance, a spiritual volcano, about to discharge itself on your earth. Be not dismayed; unrest and energy only prove that inherent life is at work. God's wheels must not clog. By all the wars and signs of the times, know[2] that the Day of the Lord is at hand, your own Lord and Christ, the indwelling and potent Christ of God. Marvel not, ye[3] must be born of water and of the spirit. This I may explain to you later. The[3] keys of the

[1] I Cor. xv. 36. [2] Matt. xxiv. 6.
[3] John iii. 5. [4] Matt. xvi. 19.

Kingdom are in your hands. Out of chaos and confusion there will come peace and order to your earth. The wars of the nations are the birth pangs of a new era, and the consciousness of the race will be lifted by the pain and agony of the refiner's fire. In the hearts of those who have attained the Christ consciousness there will be rest and glorious hope, for they shall see the new dawn arising when Christ who is our light shall reign. His kingdom cometh for ever and ever.

SECOND LESSON

BORN OF THE VIRGIN

WE were discussing the journey of spirit through matter and its goal. This knowledge is valuable to students at your stage of evolution. You have learned the truth of Being, your high calling,[1] and some of the first steps in the great path. When a traveller is going into a strange country he is sometimes brought to a seeming stop by huge tracts of forest land, tremendous rivers, and mountainous heights. The spiritual life has up to the present been one shared with others of like thought and habit as yourselves. Some of you are seeking farther on, and this means that you are called as Abraham was, alone[2] and in faith. Only

[1] Phil. iii. 14.   [2] Gen. xii. I.

122

the called see the burning bush[1] and hear the great I AM.[2] One of the obstacles we want to help you to overcome is the mystery of the Incarnation, or, as we stated at the first—the journey of the spirit. To woman[3] and to woman alone came this understanding, and it will be again revealed to the feminine in this new age. Woman is having her true place in revelation and prophecy, and to woman shall the great mystery be made known.

You have learned through previous lessons that there is perfect unity between God and man. This consciousness is slowly and surely dawning over the whole earth. Now, only by keeping this truth in mind can you comprehend our lesson. Even as God and man are one, so also there must of necessity be one only, and in this one is the all, manifesting through every channel. God is the two in one, of both natures, ever self-creative, and the ultimate end of our

[1] Ex. iii. 2.   [2] Ex. iii. 14.
[3] Luke i. 38.

race is unity. All life was symbolised by the life of Jesus Christ in every particular. He came of the perfect unity of the two natures. Mary symbolises this truth, and here we would say—lest any err by worship, or undue adoration of type or personality—that Mary was the body of flesh used for this holy manifestation, for the teaching of the world, and not because of her separate worth. Seeing that the outer self is a separation, it cannot be known as the complete Self.

The race is rising to a knowledge of the purity of God, the sinlessness and love, wherein is harmony, and some here and there are learning that the age of passion, desire, and lust is passing away. There is stealing over men's hearts the love-nature of God. It is through our love-nature that we learn the complete allness of God. He is making of the twain one flesh; this is the marriage of the two natures. Jesus Christ was born directly from the two in one—as He willingly chose to take up

the life on earth, from the beginning.
In every way He stands for our race—
man. Yes, Jesus was[1] God incarnate,
and we[2] shall be like Him. He was
creative, His seed is in[3] all, the holy
child must first be born in you ere
you can comprehend this mystery. Life
is a spiritual essence. Birth is a spiritual fact, invisible at present to mortal
eye. Jesus of Nazareth was God-Man,
coming by the path of the one body
of flesh.

Let us make quite clear that God has
always[4] been manifest in the world.
The coming of Jesus was the symbol
of the supreme wholeness and perfection
of man by the Christ of God. Learn
by this wondrous life the love of God
and the great unity. I[5] and the Father
are one.

When you have risen out of your false
belief in separateness, and know in your
heart that God is ALL in ALL, then, and

[1] I Tim. iii. 16.　　[2] I John iii. 2.
[3] Gal. iv. 19.　　[4] Acts xiv. 17.
[5] John x. 30.

then only, will you glide out of the false consciousness of sin, suffering, and pain, leaving it like a worn-out garment, rising into purer life, renewed and regenerated.

Our next lesson will be "Mind, and its possibilities."

THIRD LESSON

MIND, AND ITS POSSIBILITIES

EVERY condition of mind always brings about an outward manifestation even on the sense plane, and the separate self has power over its own environment. Thus, we will say, you think, you act, you become. Man is constantly clothing himself with[1] his thoughts, but these truths are familiar to you, and I want to lead you to the higher possibilities of the mind that is supreme in truth; the only mind, the mind of[2] Christ. The Psalmist, groping after this great truth, cries out: "Why art[3] thou so heavy, O my soul? For I will yet praise Him Who is the health of my countenance and my God."

[1]Prov. xxiii. 7.   [2]Phil. ii. 5.
[3]Ps. xliii. 5.

Around you are people in a condition of sickness, imperfection, and want, some of them Christians, as regards the following of the personal Jesus, but they have not made the great discovery of the indwelling Lord. There is no state of ignorance too low for the renewal of life and health. Those who throw off the body prematurely are just as culpable as suicides, and ignorance is not counted as innocence, since the light is in[1] all men—at some time or other the knowledge comes. I am speaking now only to readers of this book. You have no right to allow sin and death to reign in[2] your mortal bodies.

The vital question for you is—How to become alive to the mind of Christ and dead to the mind of sense? Let me here say that you have passed from death into life spiritually, but your work is less than half done if you have not conquered death[3] in your body of flesh.

[1] John i. 9.
[2] Rom. vi. 12.
[3] I Cor. xv. 26.

You are clothed in the flesh that you may manifest God, and you fail seriously if you allow anything to hide or blur the outer garment, which should manifest wholeness and love.

You thought your body must suffer and die. Still every thought and be receptive to Christ's thought. He said, I am come that they might have full, rich, abundant life.[1] Wherever Jesus went, disease dissolved into nothingness; at His touch wholeness[2] sprang up. Your body should be willingly laid down when you have learned life's lessons, and when you are ready for the interior life. You will not escape the ills of the flesh even when you kill your present body, if you have failed to obtain your earth experience; for the soul has failed to use its faculties, to acquire, to obey some divine law, and therefore loses an opportunity to express divinity, the true purpose of incarnation. There is no finer school for this experience, which we set out to gain, than

[1] John x. 10.   [2] Matt. iv. 23.

this earth life. We must enter into the Christ consciousness if we would express the body of wholeness.

Since the mind is the seat of pain, do you not see that unless you have the mind of Christ you cannot acquire it by freedom from the body of flesh only? It is more difficult to conquer on the plane of spirit, in fact, you will long to come back. Just where you are is the place to learn; therefore we who love you come to help you at your present stage, not only for your sake, but in order that the great Self, of which we are a part, may not be ignorantly hidden.

Begin by opposing sense suggestion. You are not born to suffer and decay, but are here for a purpose. There is a reason for your place in the great plan of life, and no one else can do your work. Reject the suggestion that you have diffficult circumstances, that your environment makes triumph impossible. These very conditions can be made steps of ascent; you can begin now to readjust your life. Every sense suggestion must be reasonably and carefully dealt with, not ignorantly denied, or it will crop up again and again. Therefore answer with patience and sweet reasonableness. You will find that this is the very opportunity for the higher Self to speak. Many[1] join with us, as you read these words, in prayer and strong encouragement that you fail not. Begin as we suggest, in the simplest way, to realise that it is God[2] that worketh in you to will and to do.

We hope to continue the teaching of the possibilities of mind in future lessons, and our next lesson will be "Personality." I am taking this subject because you must carefully and daily, even hourly, as you count time, follow the suggestions given, always remembering Christ in you, the Lord of all.

[1] Heb. xii. I.   [2] 2 Chron. xx. 17.

FOURTH LESSON

PERSONALITY

HUMANITY shrinks, and rightly so, from any thought of strangeness or loss, and any thought that occasions shrinking or pain should be quietly and peacefully dropped, without strife[1] or resistance. I can tell you for a certainty that you will retain your personality just as long as you need it, and you will need it much longer yet. I am allowed to say to you that the meeting with your loved ones will be sweetly familiar, a great deal better than you can imagine, for they and you will be enriched by the love between you. Your loss is always gain. You can help them by your love and prayer, and they help you; think often of them. Bless them and become

[1] Matt. v. 39.

conscious of unity, which is a blessed reality. There is nothing untoward or strange; you are here just what you have made yourselves, and they who love you would not have you with them until you have finished. In fact, you are near them now, but the veil or covering is over you at present.

Love—Love—Love. This is a potent force. It would not meet the demands of your present nature to arrive suddenly at the end of being, since everything in God's plan is in perfect order. There must be gradual unfoldment and gentle awakening; even after the spirit ceases to need its personal form, it can always resume it at will. Paul,[1] who was allowed to enter the interior realms, tells you that the inner man is[2] renewed day by day in an identity peculiarly your own, and exactly resembling you as you appeared, except that you have added the spiritual qualities, refining and defining all the highest and best. This, too, is a covering or resurrection body,

[1] 2 Cor. xii. 2.　　　　　[2] 2 Cor. iv. 16.

and it is clothed in[1] white raiment to appear before mortal eyes.

As your Scriptures tell you repeatedly, the continuity of life is[2] no more broken when the breath leaves the body than is the continuity of child life broken by the incident of birth. It is the means by which life is liberated, becoming more intense. Memory[3] exists, although we have learned the power to dissolve into nothingness—this is true forgetfulness—all that is not of use. But I would have you know that you are greater than your form, that you have no limit, that you take limitations for purposes at present hidden from you, that true personality is not the fleshly form or a separate body, but, by reason of its greatness, is best manifested in part.

Paul, who had learned this mystery, tells you plainly that "the body is for the Lord, and the Lord[4] for the body," therefore it is quite clear that the body or form is only a part of the great whole,

[1]John xx. 12.　　[2]2 Tim. i. 10.
[3]Luke xvi. 28.　　[4]I Cor. vi. 13.

the mystic body of Christ. Paul also had revealed to him the omnipresence of man, as he was present in spirit with the Church of Corinth while his body[1] was visible in another place. Always bear in mind that to us there is neither time nor space.

I told you at the beginning that your Scriptures could reveal the highest, and you will find more and more that we only present to you in a new light the truth which was from the beginning, so that you may see life from higher standpoints, with renewed vision, new hopes, and moving in loftier spheres of thought and experience.

Now you begin to see that the Lord Christ possesses the body of flesh, through which you choose to manifest;[2] and there is no reason why it should not readily respond, unless you yield to the great enemy, the false belief in separateness. This enemy is symbolised in the story of the Garden of Eden, the separation from God. The

[1] I Cor. v. 3. [2] I Cor. iii. 16; I Cor. vi. 19.

lower self would become even as the gods, though in the words—"Hear, O¹ Israel, the Lord thy God is One Lord" —it was taught that we are one, that separate or outer forms never can finally overrule the One God. God requires perfection; therefore if we would rise to this consciousness we must begin with our lower self to bring it into obedience and subjection to the One Ruler; and as we do this we learn what our true personality is. We shall not accomplish this great purpose without constant watchfulness² and wholeheartedness,³ giving all to gain all, ready at every turn to sacrifice the lower self, that we may become selfless and free.

¹Deut. vi. 4.   ²Mark xiii. 37.
³Mark xii. 30.

FIFTH LESSON

THE TRUE SELF

"Let him deny himself and follow Me"

HOW often we have to remind you of the truth you have already learnt! Spirit is the only substance; exactly as the sap is the true life of the tree, so also your spiritual being is the cause of your natural existence. You can never impart a truth until it has become alive within yourself. We have many things to tell you about the life here, but at present your highest good is to learn the truths best applicable to your present conditions.

When I speak of the wholeness of the race and the mystical body, I do not want to give you wrong ideas about your individual responsibility. Each member is a complete worker. What you see on the plane of the senses is to us shadowy, vague, and often meaningless. You are to make real, to create, to bring into existence, spiritual realities by living on the only real plane of life. This is to[1] bring in the new heaven and the new earth. Your spiritual eyes will open gradually, not into an unfamiliar environment, but into an intensely real life, wherein dwelleth[2] righteousness.

We are working all over the world in bands to establish true unity and brotherhood. We shall succeed if you will unite with us. Is it not worth while? True unity is not to separate heaven from earth, but to bring the kingdom of heaven on to earth. For this we labour and pray—watch and wait —and we shall never cease until the Lord Christ has come to His own, the Christ of God who spake with the lips of Jesus; the Christ of God who dwells within, the great deliverer of mankind from the

[1] Rev. xxi. I.   [2] 2 Peter iii. 13.

bondage of sin, flesh, and the world of sense. For the Son of man must indeed be lifted up,[1] and the false man of sense become as nought, that we all may be one—for Christ is God. Clearly you see the importance of denying self and following the voice and guidance of Christ!

In the morning of your day commence by cleansing your heart from within (the cleansing of the body follows as his shadow follows a man in the full sunshine). First cast out false thinking, prejudice, thoughts of sickness, fear and pain, by true reasoning and simple, childlike faith in God. As you rise, your thoughts should be of strength, love, a strong desire to bless. Now follows your prayer, a free and full consecration of all for good, that God only may be glorified, a prayer of steadfast assurance—Take no[2] thought what ye shall eat or what ye shall put on. The life is more than meat, the body than raiment. It is true that God will

[1] John xii. 32.   [2] Matt. vi. 25.

supply[1] your every need. In all your thoughts and deeds, your intercourse with personalities, remember that you are on the plane of spirit, seeking first the[2] kingdom of God, the only reality.

Oh, you are rich beyond human language! Leave your chamber "strong in[3] the Lord and in the power of His might." Let your whole being join in the only true life-work—"That they[4] all may be one."

Amen, Amen, Amen

[1]Phil. iv. 19.
[3]Eph. vi. 10.
[2]Matt. vi. 33.
[4]John xvii. II.

SIXTH LESSON

THE TRUE SELFISHNESS

B^{E[1]} of good courage, for all is well. God dwelleth in you, and this is the chief eternal truth.

I know you are progressing because already you can command right thoughts and dismiss inharmonious ones. Results will follow, and now you will learn discrimination. It is not given to all to be able to judge others, but content yourself, when tempted to judge, with praying for them, and as you evolve, your prayers will be fraught with healing, because you are learning to pray aright. Be of good courage. Evil is friendly and has a beneficent purpose. Man becomes God-like because he rises through and out of evil, just as the

[1] Ps. xxvii. 14.

plants emerge from the soil. Every good is closely imitated in the false dream world, and one of the imitations is called selfishness. This is a divine instinct, and you cannot and should not uproot it, but learn always that these delusions of sense have behind them a truth of God. Let us discover the true and holy selfishness.

Man's first instinct is self-interest, self-protection. Even in spiritual things you are constantly seeking to acquire for yourself. You require healing of the body, a rich mind, a true life. This is a God-given instinct, and you are to get, but learn that to get is to give. The true law of giving is to benefit all, and thus you bring good to your Self; which, remember, is the great and only Self.

Let us begin by a simple explanation. I use the language of earth that you may understand, for you know already that material things have no real existence, that your thought of them is their only reality. Do you desire health of body? Let us teach you how to obtain it, the true way. You begin at once to send out healing currents to someone in a lower condition than yourself, and immediately you have made a pathway by which your own shall come to you. Your first thought, I see, is, how can I heal when sick myself? The first time you try it, you will understand that the very effort of faith required is the beginning of your own healing, and the larger love going out to others doubles your own joy in the long run.

True[1] getting is always by way of sacrifice. This is a simple thing to know, but it is the key to all true healing, of mind, body, or estate; for all you have truly given you will receive double, but you do not render to the Lord that which costs[2] you nothing. In the sight of God, no gift has been blessed to your own soul unless you have willingly given from your heart and blessed the gift by your love. You may have wealth untold, though unmanifest

[1] Acts xx. 35. [2] 2 Sam. xxiv. 24.

to mortal eye. A good practice each day is to bless and heal everyone in the house. Begin at once, knowing only the great Self, remembering the need of all in the house. Your own Lord will reveal each need; be resolute, be positive, and, above all, full of hope and love. If the unseen become visible at such times, include them; only send out, give, give, give. I tell you that this is your real getting, your real healing.

The spirit reveals to you more and more. Do you not see that I am helping you to one of the richest possessions; that you may become a centre of healing; spirit, the pure flame, burning up the dross; the soul, the link, holding all the physical powers; and the body, showing the beauty[1] of the Lord, the true beauty[2] of Holiness.

Again I ask that you put these lessons into practice.

[1] Ps. xc. 17.　　　　　[2] I Chron. xvi. 29.

SEVENTH LESSON

DWELL DEEP

YOU are spirit, soul, and body. The spirit, the innermost, is clothed upon by the soul. The body is the vehicle for manifestation. Your wholeness depends upon the one consciousness, and the active co-operation of soul and body. Knowing only God brings into operation hidden laws, at present unknown to you. You develop spiritual powers which have hitherto lain dormant, and your whole being begins to live. Hearing, seeing, touch, and the power to communicate belong to the soul; they are transmitted to a denser body for a divine purpose. The soul has great responsibilities, and everything depends upon her obedience to the Lord and Master, and to her transfer of spiritual desire to the outer body. More than this, by true living you send forth spiritual vibrations, currents of blessing and healing, and all are helped by your radiant and pure environment.

Every spiritual desire, expressed through the outer body, goes on and obeys a higher law; it is never lost. Never mind if you do not see results. I tell you the result of every noble thought expressed has far-reaching effects, and you will know one day that the faintest longing desire has been satisfied.

When you meditate or pray, it is the soul and not the body that opens to the spirit; mind-wandering or lack of earnestness means that the brain is not co-operating with the soul. See to it that you are definite; and think, speak, act from the innermost of yourself. Your soul is your real identity. It is You.

The soul thinks, breathes, acts from the spirit, and should make perfect the outer body. Wherever this is not so, the soul has failed in its obedience to spirit. If this disobedience takes place, you will find that the passing out of the flesh does not mean that the soul will then function freely; for disuse of the spiritual medium means coma, arrested growth, sleep. Awake![1] thou that sleepest, Christ dwells within.

When you have ceased to need the body you will give back the atoms, purified and transmuted by the divine life. Do not repress life, but express it. There is nothing either in or out of the flesh that can hinder the disciple who is at one with the will of God.

[1] Eph. v. 14.

EIGHTH LESSON

UNFOLDMENT FROM WITHIN

THE soul has entered your present body that it may express God's meaning through this medium, also because the soul has need of certain experiences. The body, too, must be rightly valued, seeing that it exists for a divine purpose; but it is only of value when it takes its true place in the divine order. The soul is the sheath[1] of the spirit, the clothing of man, who is for the time veiled in flesh.

Man becomes God-like only through experience and discipline. This can be understood in your present period of life by the comparison between an innocent, happy child and a happy, ripe old age;

[1] Dan. vii. 15, margin.

the one is ignorantly happy and the
other has matured and unfolded through
knowledge and suffering. Both are happy,
but the difference is very great. Your
present earth experience is the most
beneficial state for your present healthy
development.

The mind functions from the soul.
Before man awakes to self-knowledge
the sense mind has ruled. All the cells
in your body have their centre, their
mind; the grey matter of the brain is not
the only centre for the sensation of mind.
When ruled by The Christ mind they are
flooded by the great intelligence in
every part, each doing its work perfectly.
But the soul of man awakes in a body
that has formed a kingdom of its own,
and a warfare begins. This is the very
period of your life at which I would help
you: we call it the transitional, and it is
a time when you need all your faith
and hope, for the body is so frequently
unable to respond to the new king, and
seems for a while to fail. Have faith:
believe me, it is true that once you have

passed this stage, you gain what you will never lose; you also rise into a higher cycle, and have opportunities for greater work.

It is at this very point that, from being the healthy, uncivilised man, you become the spiritually healthy God-Man. You fail perhaps to become your ideal at once, but you will surely win. Obey the highest within you, and never let the sense mind rule you. For this reason I say that you cannot believe in what you see; you are conscious that you are about to manifest all things anew. This is a slow process, since false thinking has brought about false conditions. As an illustration, melancholy or depression causes acidity in the blood, and can only be cast out by its opposite—joy or hope. Remedies from without can do good for a time only. The inner man[1] should be daily re-newed by spirit, the one reality. It is not meet that the last should be first. Spirit rules. Love and harmony should

[1] 2 Cor. iv. 16.

prevail, not warfare and strife. Teach the body that its highest good is obedience to its Lord. Now you know enough to be able to say—Christ reigns in me.

Rise in harmony—spirit, soul, and body reaching the eternal consciousness, which is unchanging, holy. You have learned that this is not the case with the lower self; the sense mind being changefull, evanescent, susceptible, to other influences, other minds. Now you are wholeness, true health and unchanging thought. This is the path to unity with the two worlds. Christ in you, bringing life and[1] immortality to light. You will receive the inner illumination. You are learning what a glorious thing your unfoldment is, warmed into growth by the interior sun. The soul has a real work to do in your body through the mind of Christ. Rejoice that you have burst the outer covering of the seed, that by an immutable law you must rise.

[1] 2 Tim i. 10.

Sit in silence, and slowly repeat the
Lord's Prayer. Its spiritual meaning
will arise in you. For thine is the kingdom, the power, and the glory. Amen.
Amen. Amen.

NINTH LESSON

THE SOUL

I SHOULD like to continue our dis-
cussion on the soul, for I rejoice
to know that you realise the spiritual
world to be here. You will live in it
more and more, learning that spirit
is true substance, and that you function
truly from your luminous body, holding
within yourself all you need.

Wherever you see beauty, truth, or
goodness, it is God finding expression,
and you will see them where you least
expect when dwelling on the spiritual
plane, and much that seems to the
natural eye good, beautiful, and true
you will prove to be false imitations
of the real. Music, art, poetry are
expressions of God. All genius is God
revealing Himself; by the very revela-

tion, the soul refines the outer body, which should be as clay in the hands of the potter.[1]

All states of existence, now, and in the future, are determined by the inner life and its expression. It is not enough to know that you possess the indwelling power to become the eternal Christ. Your real work, like that of Jesus, is to express[2] God. Your environment is the outcome of your mind and thought. Heaven and hell are states of existence you make for yourself here and now. Your fall away from truth is caused by the soul's separation from God's thought, and by following the false self-consciousness. Listen to your own Lord and Christ, who brings deliverance[3] to the captive and sight to the blind, who redeemeth thy life from destruction.[4]

The seven creative days are experiences within yourself. God speaks the word of power when He says, "Let

[1]Jer. xviii. 6.   [2]John xiv. 9.
[3]Luke iv. 18.   [4]Ps. ciii. 4.

there be light,[1] and the light shineth from within.'' The dividing of the[2] waters is the separation of the divine and the human, the firmament symbolising the Heavenly-Divine, and the seas the Earthly-Human. The separation of sea and land means the first state of receptivity, to express clearly that land (mind) is free and awaiting God's manifestation. And God said, Let the earth[3] (mind) bring forth, and God says within you, to your soul: bring forth, manifest, express My thought.

Then you read: God gave the two lights, the[4] greater and the lesser. These symbolise the lights of the two understandings—human and divine. The seas are[5] fruitful on the fifth day, thus proving the creativeness of mind and the birth of ideas. Then we read of larger growth, larger idea, till we come finally to ourselves—man in the image of God,[6] God's idea. You have

[1] Gen. i. 3.
[2] Gen. i. 6, 7.
[3] Gen. i. II.
[4] Gen. i. 16.
[5] Gen. i. 20.
[6] Gen. i. 26.

not entered into the seventh period yet.[1]
It is one of great delight and triumph.
Read this for yourselves with the spiritual
understanding.

Each soul makes its own Heaven,
and there is a sense in which each
created being augments Heaven by its
own created environment. By your
rebirth into the spiritual kingdom,
heaven itself becomes greater. In this
sense you can understand better what
I mean when I tell you that all are bene-
fitted by one, because you are a part of
all. I use the language of earth, but
you have spiritual discernment.[2] We
can never find true language to express
Heaven and God, since the first is a
state of consciousness, and the second
infinity.

I have given you these three lessons
on the one subject, as it is good for you
to live according to divine and spiritual
law. With all thy getting, get[3] wisdom.
When the soul sees and knows, life

[1]Gen. ii. 2.   [2]I Cor. ii. 14.
[3]Prov. iv. 7.

appears orderly, and the body of flesh sensibly obedient. Be[1] patient; much more shall be revealed. The kingdom of heaven is open to all believers.

Love, Peace, Joy.

[1] Jas. v. 7, 8.

PART III

DIVINE HUMANITY

FIRST LESSON

I IN THEM

I WANT to unfold to your understanding something of the meaning
of God immanent and God transcend-
ent. God and man are not separated,
and never have been.[1] After our lesson
on the mind and soul you are quite
aware of the oneness and unity of
life. You are in every living thing.
You are round about everything that is.
You cannot separate yourself from anything that lives, moves, and has its
being. You are in the rock, the crystal,
in every bud and twig, in all places
at all times. You have always been.
The sense of separateness is false understanding, and brings only confusion of
mind.

[1] John xvii. 21.

Is not this feeling of unity more than
a relation to God? Is it not the One
speaking and breathing through all
forms—all Creation—the creator and the
created? How sayest thou: "Show us
the Father"? "He that hath seen Me,
hath seen the Father."[1] Oh, priceless
truth, now our privilege and joy to enter
into! "I and[2] the Father are one."

How are we going to live, so that
this knowledge may be used for all?
You dwell in the uttermost parts of
the earth, you have your responsibility
there, here, and everywhere. You are
not without a witness, and you know
nothing but the one good, one will;
not a union of spirit with parent spirit,
but an at-one-ment. Knowing only one
Lord—one God—one Christ—this is
not a mystery to you any longer. The
race is unfolding, and you are unfolding; and just as you yield to truth
and love, so all are helped. I cannot
put this too strongly, for in it is the
answer to all the seeming mystery of

[1] John xiv. 9.　　　　　　　　[2] John x. 30.

pain and the sorrows of life. Surely[1]
He hath borne our griefs and carried
our sorrows, and is doing this even now.

Will you reverently consider why you
seem to be a limited part? Is it not
because you have looked upon God as
apart from yourself, thought of the indwelling Christ as Jesus of Nazareth?
Do you not see for yourself how childlike has been your understanding?
Your dependence upon someone, something, proved your childlike consciousness; and even as a child learns to say:
I am myself, so will the whole human
race say, as we now say together: I in
you and you in Me. I am Myself.
This understanding is putting Christ on
the throne, lifting Him to where he
deals with error and sin as a thing
outside Himself. The truth dawns,
and the inner Christ reveals to man
his birthright, his true power, and
henceforth he becomes one with, for
and through all. Think for a moment
how you dishonour Jesus as teacher

[1]Isa. liii. 4.

if you hold Him responsible for the forgiveness of your ignorance. Hath He not said: All that[1] the Father hath is yours, is mine? He hath also given you the key, the power of appropriation by faith.

[1]Luke xv. 31; John xvi. 15; I Cor. iii. 21; Matt xxviii. 18; Luke x. 19.

SECOND LESSON

"THOU IN ME"

KEEP in mind the previous chapter, and you will be led back to it and find that all your life is going to teach you that the God-Man Christ is all in all. This truth has to be made one with the outermost limits of creation, just as a leaf learns by drawing from its source its oneness—more than unity—with the tree. There is a condition of consciousness in everything that lives. The real you knows everything about itself, but the leaf or seeming unit can only learn slowly, by its life of dependence and unfoldment, its own place and meaning. Every atom contains the whole. The whole of God is in the blade of grass. Try to banish the thought of distance or space, and know that what you see contains within it its true life; the thought is within every expression.

Your first and lowest consciousness of life was movement. Your highest is love. The seed thought is always hidden within every phase of life through which you merge; it moves, quickens, and brings forth seed (thought). This is true of all creation. Your first movement was in secret,[1] yea, in the lowest parts of the earth. This is symbolised in every physical birth; the whole of creation is manifest to the seer. The truths of life are simple and open. I do not wish to cause you vain speculation, but we desire to be of real practical use to you at the stage of unfoldment where you now are. However low in the scale of evolution—that is, spiritual evolution—a soul is, it can be perfect of its kind, and should be free from sin, sickness, and death. This is our glorious message for you. We would have you know yourselves. Get back to the cause.

[1] Ps. cxxxix. 15.

Why are people suffering and sinful? Because they willingly choose to dwell in a divided consciousness of good and evil. Whoever for even a second has seen that there is[1] no evil, has passed from death to life. He has entered the Heaven of Heavens, he has seen God. The Fall is a thing of the present. It is a false understanding.

Why have we tolerated this consciousness, seeing that God cannot fail? The real you has never tolerated it. There is only one consciousness really; it is deep within yourself all the time; it always has been, and now is around you; and because of it and its livingness you are shaking off the shadow of ignorance—a condition of growth—and rising into pure being. In the great process you will know that sin and ignorance are less than the morning mists now being dispelled by the inner sun, the fire of the love-life. To become aware, while in the shadow, of the reality of this one true life is the solution of everything, for

[1] Isa. xxxiii. 15.

with this true understanding you must know that all is well for ever. That you are one with this movement means that you are emerging into fulness and freedom. See how it is lifting the whole race! We see its potent healing power everywhere; we rejoice with you. You are entering into the kingdom of life and light. Death and sin are conquered now and for ever.

In our next lesson we will discuss the way of ascent from your present condition.

Peace and joy and the sweet fellowship of the heavenly host be yours, as you consider these truths.

Nothing is impossible to him that believeth.

THIRD LESSON

"SEEK AND YE SHALL FIND"

THE question may be asked: Why are so many people still in bondage even with this knowledge? We are in earnest, and are willing to be and do what we can. It is good for you to give your heart to the understanding of wisdom. Knowledge is not understanding. To know God we must be God-like. Because we long for perfection, we are already at its beginnings. Do not regard any of these things as distant or outside yourselves: that is the spirit of separateness. Let us meet the seeming difficulties together, the weights and hindrances of your everyday life, for the truth will[1] set you free.

Many of you seem to be in bondage

[1] John viii. 32.

to the climate, to lack of heat or to unevenness of temperature. Your bodies are subject to many influences. I too suffered in this way, and I would gladly help you with my experience. How could I understand that what I needed was within? I thought it necessary to be warmly clad, to avoid chill, and to take food to sustain life. Ah! if I could only show you for a minute a spiritual being who has passed this stage, you would know beyond all doubt that Christ is the[1] bread of life, the true daily bread, nourishing both soul and body, able to supply your every need.

When you awake in the morning you look outside and see cold; now you both see and feel cold. You must see before you feel a truth or a falsehood; this is a law. We shall straightway begin to reverse the order. You will look within and see only God, you will feel and understand God. Your feeblest effort in this direction must have its reward.

[1] John vi. 35.

Read this truth into every detail of the day, and live in the assurance that God cannot fail. See reality, God, behind every shadow. As you go into the outer, cast out fear. Be not anxious, and the very elements will be at one with you. This is the rule of the spiritual. Your whole supply for every need is within yourself. The day is at hand when man, on the earth, will be a true spiritual being. Even now you have expressed yourself in the present phase, and the God-Man is seeking a higher form of manifestation; but all must co-operate, and you are learning the laws of the spiritual kingdom for this end, that sorrow and sighing[1] may flee away, that the sons and daughters of God may hunger no[2] more. Your responsibility is great, but your work is for eternity. Do not lose heart. Be of good courage. The work may seem slow, but God is in it. The result in yourself will be first a sense of command, and later you will smile at your

[1] Isa. xxxv. 10.   [2] Rev. vii. 16.

old fears and limitations, for you will be at home and at rest in any climate or circumstance.

Do you not see for yourself how your thought has been concerned with your dependence upon material warmth, food, and sustenance? Later you will put these in their true place, and life will open out its treasure.[1] At present your whole time and thought are given to caring for the daily outer life. Think what the spiritual being with its higher faculties could enter into if you gave half as much time and thought to the true life!

Live simply. Take no anxious thought for the things of to-day. Let the dead bury[2] their dead. Follow ME. I am within.

[1] Deut. xxviii. 12.　　　　[2] Matt. viii. 22.

FOURTH LESSON

"THE KNOWLEDGE OF GOD SHALL COVER THE EARTH"

THE day of the Lord is at hand, is here. Truly the Lord Christ has come in great glory. The signs are in earth and sky. Lift up your heads. The King of[1] glory has come in. This is the wonder, the silence of this new birth.

What does it mean for you? The consciousness of Christ is dawning in every lowly heart. The supreme man Christ is on the throne, and darkness is[2] under His feet. God tells this blessed secret to the dwellers in the innermost, that they may carry the tidings to the very outermost. The Lord our God is One Lord, even

[1] Ps. xxiv.   [2] Ps. xviii. 9.

Christ. There is something for you to do in this work, but all good, all knowledge is within oneself. The real need for help is great. We see souls imprisoned in limitations, thirsting for living waters. My people would die for lack[1] of understanding. Man is divine, and God is ever in the midst.

Your true consciousness is the knowledge that One and One only fills all[2] space. When you silently think of this you will know that in this understanding, in this continual realisation, true freedom lies. You will cast off everything alien to this; nay, you will transmute the very sins and ignorances into the pure gold and wealth of life. These must be the healing of the self by the Self, the forgiveness, the whole redemption from your Christ, your indwelling Lord. You are in all and through all, in every place, since hidden within yourself is the centre of all worlds.

As you write these words we are

[1] Hos. iv. 6.   [2] Jer. xxiii. 24.

near you, and many would like to come back and tell you the glorious news, to open your eyes that you may see in very truth—"There am[1] I in the midst." So far you have understood clearly the one Self of all, when you have looked within, but now we will try to look out upon seemingly separate personalities and still see the One only. To recognise the one Lord in all is to lift them into the consciousness of the Christ, and this is just what the spiritually taught are doing. You must each do your part where you are.

Help souls to cast out fear. Fear is one of your foes. In one way or another you allow this false condition to cloud your vision and drag down your spirits. Get rid of[2] fear for yourself and for others. There is absolutely nothing to fear. The indwelling Christ is Lord supreme.

Remind yourself constantly of your true nature. Declare that the light dispels darknes, and see this law in action.

[1] Matt. xviii. 20.   [2] I John iv. 18.

I no longer,[1] but Christ the Lord God
omnipotent reigneth. See what this
little enemy fear has done, a very fox,
spoiling[2] the vine. In your immediate
environment, the body, fear affects its
circulation, digestion, and gastric juices.
I only use these words so that we
may swiftly ascend to a higher plane.
Fear not. There is none other[3] God
but ME.

Once rid the race of fear; and love,
joy, peace, will spring up. Now this
must positively be done in each one of
you. In fact, the universe has been conquered when *you* have won. Your
own Christ has conquered sin and
death.

Face life and circumstances with the
certainty of the I AM with you and in
you. Only thus will you honour God.
Try from this moment to forget the
small you, false and shadowy, and cast
it off for ever. Here I would say that
only love is Lord. You can fill the

[1] Gal. ii. 20.   [2] Song ii 15.
[3] Isa. xlv.

whole mentality with love thoughts, so making a rich soil for the growth of good. You have nothing to fear. You are in God and God is in you.

Cleanse[1] your hearts, and not your garments. From within must the true forgiveness arise, and not from without. Be clean every whit, whole and perfect. Be positive; know that you must make your circumstances, and not wait for events and then act. You are blind and miserable till your inner eyes, "the eyes of[2] the understanding," are opened. "It is high time to awake out of[3] sleep." Use these God-given powers for the good of everyone. There is nothing outside God. God and man are one. Confidence and trust are[3] the antidotes for anxiety and fear.

[1] Joel ii. 13.
[2] Eph. i. 18; Job xxxii. 8; Prov. xx. 27.
[3] Rom. xii. II.   [4] Isa. xxxii. 17, xxx. 15.

FIFTH LESSON

THE WILL OF GOD

WHAT a long time it takes us to understand the will of God!

You often use the phrase, "I have made up my mind." This has a great deal of meaning, if you pause to consider it, for in that very process you begin to bring into manifestation the desire of the mind. Thus you say: "I see a wrong condition in my mind, my mentality, my circumstances; I will make up my mind, this shall not be." You mentally set in motion the forces of the universe, seen and unseen, to accomplish your will.

You see, it is impossible to live carelessly or lightly on the spiritual plane, and these lessons would be of no use to anyone who has not been aroused to true spiritual consciousness, the consciousness of the divine humanity, the I AM. How can the will of God be expressed except through life, through humanity, in the hearts and minds of beings who exist in Himself? Therefore know that the will of God is operative in yourself.

Then how is it that the things we will and desire do not come to us, you may ask.

Because deep down in all your desires, thoughts, and purposes there is an undercurrent, as it were, the thought within the thought, the desire within the desire, and what you most truly desire is always at the root of all your fleeting impressions and moods of the moment. Have you not often felt that the very thing you desire is not for your eternal good? Well, that very glimmer, that faint suggestion, is from the Self of you that is making your life. You know within yourself the very quality, the very experiences best suited for your highest good. Once you give full play to this

subtle suggestion behind[1] all your thinking, you are one with the will of God,
which is your own will. This is the
voice of the spirit, heed its whisperings.
Do not sin against the Holy Ghost, or
you will lose eye and ear and become
blind and deaf. On the plane of the
senses this is most disastrous, because
you are just where you are to do the
will of God. It is your meat and[2] drink.
So delicate and so subtle is this holy
inner voice that you must be very quiet
and meek, if you would hear[3] it. Let
Jesus speak to you again and again,
read the Gospels until you are led more
and more to remove the veil which
hides you from your true Self. I have
only answered your question, but hope
to speak to you again on this subject.

Peace, Heavenly Grace. God lives
in you, He is your life.

[1] Isa. xxx. 21.　　　　　　　　[2] John iv. 34.
[3] Ps. xxv. 9.

SIXTH LESSON

WORKERS TOGETHER WITH GOD

THERE really is no such thing as space. For you, as for us, the spiritual law of attraction operates, but your consciousness of limitation, of distance, makes you blind and deaf to a great extent. At a later period of your unfoldment, to desire is to possess. Thus, if we wish to see you, our thought is a vital force, we are in your actual presence immediately, we are so close to you. Thought is so potent, so swift; every thought of ours becomes an outward expression; although you may not see it, you cannot think without a result. Be very careful that you think from the spiritual plane. The phenomena of time and sense are like children's toys to us. They will be discarded as you

181

dwell in the higher consciousness. What divides us now is simply and only that you are not dwelling in, not breathing, seeing, hearing from the spiritual plane. Every effort to rise helps another; but see to it that you are watchful, vigilant, purposeful, and loving.

You partake of the inflow and outflow of the breath of God. This is best described as waves, impelled by an irresistible law, and your whole planet is continually being swept over by this mighty healing breath. I am explaining this for purposes of healing, and hope to explain later that there are periods of outflow and recall. We wish you to breathe forth your healing currents in unison with the almighty good. Your co-operation is necessary for individual needs.

Noon and sunrise are good times for raising conditions of false consciousness into the great One, especially the conditions known to you as feverish and nervous, or the consciousness of weakness. Other cases I hope to explain as

I see you coming into contact; but previous to the expression of your desire for the healing of the body and a change of circumstances, *breathe out a strong positive assurance of man's unity with God.* Your highest good is to banish the idea of separation from God.

Bands of us are striving to influence men and women to free your land of asylums, reformatories, prisons, and similar places. Their inmates could be helped and healed so much more easily if they could be brought in contact with those who have learned the great truths we come to teach. We do not give these lessons for any other reason than to help your world, which we love. We hope to be of practical use in freeing your world from suffering, which is caused by ignorance. By this we do not mean that you escape discipline, but how can you begin to learn your real purpose for being if you are in bondage to false conditions? God did not purpose that your life should be spent in overcoming false conditions. He has a magnificent purpose, a part for you to take in His work.

God bless you and keep you alive unto Himself and dead to sin. Amen.

SEVENTH LESSON

THE CREATIVE ENERGY

IT is the silent, creative great One, dwelling in the abyss of each, in whom we live and have our being. I am being taken within the centre of life. Again I am in the centre of power, but this time I remember that I have always been. The process of creation is always present; it is not a past series of events. There is no sense of past or future, but of a continuous present. I have already described the great, silent energy and the lack of colour and sound when in the centre, but this time the desire of life is upon me, the sense of lack. I desire beauty and colour. I am the positive one, and the virility and strength of the atmosphere around me lacks its opposite.

With the desire I will, and soon the will, which is the producer, directs my forces. There is a new power about me. I am surrounded by a great arc of light, and I become conscious of a heart within myself. I love, I will! The arc, which was of a varying shade of gold, slowly becomes roseate and glowing; the electrons of light are no longer colourless, but softened and shaded by pink. Love expresses the beautiful in colour. I am answered in myself. I am both positive and negative, male and female; and out of this consciousness, beauty of form and shade seem born; yet as I write this I know that perfection has always been, though I bring it into evidence by my will and desire. Colours surround me, and millions of shades seem to evolve from three—red, blue, and yellow. They harmonise and blend, and the place seems full of sound and form. I have desired, I have willed. The colours emit the sound, and soon I see the forms of flowers. These colours cannot be seen on the physical plane, though they are full of light and breath. As you see, this is extremely difficult to describe, as also for you to imagine, but the colours breathe and live, and are inter-related to sound and form. There seems no division between the moving shades and the appearance of elegant and delightful shapes. Truly I am in a place of beauty, which is born out of the two in one. There is a sense of completeness, a harmony of many parts. The great energy is softened by beauty, and love is the breath of this life.

The teacher speaks. You could not bear this for long, and the meaning will unfold to you. One single drop of dew contains what you have seen with the eye of the soul. The Creator is in the atom. Yes, truly, the whole of God is in the blade of grass. By this know that space is a meaningless word on the true plane of being.

Everything is in the universal soul; the Christ mind alone comprehends.

The one Self is creative, having both natures.

In heaven there is neither marrying nor giving in marriage. This is the highest consciousness of Christ.

EIGHTH LESSON

GOD THE ONLY LIFE

I WANT to tell you how real, how true it is, that nothing exists outside God, and I can best help you by the description of an experience of my own. Life both here and there is a constant unfoldment, always fresh, a continual revelation.

I have already told you of my entrance into the spiritual world, and now may I speak of one of my steps into a greater fulness of God, into life more abundant? I had learnt many things, the spiritual faculties were quickened, and I was always learning that our especial need is to have greater capacities for God, to do as Paul says continually—"Yield[1] yourselves unto God." It was most

[1] Rom. vi. 13.

wonderful to discover that my thought
instantly produced an outer environment; in fact, my thought came into
being at once. For instance, I desire
quiet for meditation—I am instantly
in a grove and all is stillness, inviting
repose. I think music—and at once
I hear sublimest strains, ravishing and
melodious. I am satisfied—the music
gently ceases. Truly, eye hath not seen,
nor ear heard, all that awaits us when
we are in God. I desire to help, and
I am sent to people who are climbing
up; and oh! the joy of helping them
to their own. This is my longing desire
for you. Be ye holy[1] (healthy), for I
am holy (healthy), says God. Happiness
and health and all good is God. There
is no secret initiation, no mystery in
God. You only need the heart of the
child to[2] enter the kingdom. It is true
in a beautiful sense that there is nothing
hidden which shall not be revealed.
All things are open and are yours.
You are not always able to understand

[1] Lev. xix. 2.   [2] Mark x. 15.

because you are not sufficiently evolved; but never forget that all is yours, for ye are God's.

Even this exquisite joy around me, even the knowledge that my thought made me, did not seem enough, and I longed intensely[1] for God above all else, until I realised that nothing but the Infinite could satisfy me. This thought, this desire, was not answered in the usual way, but one of the shining ones who go in and out among us stood beside me and said, "Are you ready for the cleansing waters? Your prayer is heard." At the same time the spirit within repeated the familiar words: "Ye shall[2] surely find ME." "Yes, yes," I said, "all for God," and I fell on my knees in an attitude of prayer. Then began the cleansing by the waters from the River of God. From within there arose a cleansing stream, that made me aware of its workings in my heart. My limitations must go. I, who thought I

[1]Ps. xlii. 1.   [2]Jer. xxix. 13.

possessed relatives, friends, home, must learn that God must enlarge my heart with greater loves, more friendships.

There are no limitations where God is, no claiming of personalities. God is all. The waters were bitter, but you must do this for the great gain. Your ideas and thoughts are not God's thoughts, nor are your ways God's ways.[1] Ah, it is true, and it will be your eternal good to know this now. Everything that seemed peculiarly my own was simply swept away until I was as nothing, and longing only for God. The Angel spake again with great love and tenderness—"Thou shalt know thyself by this test: art thou content to be nothing, and know nothing?" With great faltering I answered "Yes." The reply came, "Know God, and thou shalt BE." I think there was a long time of quiet. I seemed to become conscious of fresh surroundings. I seemed in the centre of the worlds, in a place of strength; I was conscious of the heart of love, far above my under-

[1] Isa. lv. 8.

standing—the rest and comfort of a great strength, and yet I suppose the best description for you is that I seemed in the atmosphere of God—knowing nothing but God—wanting nothing but good; and yet aware that it would take me aeons to understand, to know and grow in this heavenly consciousness. Soon I saw our earth, I saw the blindness of men; though dwelling in this wondrous love they were content to live in shadow, in pain. "Lord, I must go to them, I must tell them," I thought. The voice of the Spirit spoke within—"I' am God, and beside me there is none else." "Amen, Amen, Amen," I answered.

To dwell consciously in God is to inbreathe and outbreathe harmony, and love. I am without limits, I revel in freedom, I cannot think sin, sickness, or death except to remove them; they have become to me less than vapour. God is all in all, and no one can be outside God. Even your very stones and rocks are interpenetrated by the

'Isa. xlv. 18.

God-life. "Awake, thou that sleepest, arise from the dead"; "Christ is[1] the light of the world." Oh for a thousand voices to proclaim the truth that nothing *is* but God! Rise out of your false, shadowy consciousness and mount into the consciousness of love. "Truly He maketh my[2] feet like hinds' feet." I know that in me the Christ has ascended to His Father; henceforth "the Father and I are one." In me the Trinity of the Three are one, and yet three.

Spirit is substance, nothing can be real except God; but joy of joys, as I met relatives, friends, and dear ones, I knew, how more than ever they were mine beyond thought of loss or separation! All I had lost was the *fear of losing.* God's thought is the only reality; the world is God's thought. You are yet to learn that all realities are in God's thought. You are to express them. Rise, dear heart, and take your place with us, that you may know God only,

[1] John viii. 12.   [2] Hab. iii. 19.

just where you are. Love never[1] faileth. Begin now. This is the true way to bring in light and love, conquering death by the sacrifice of the body of sense, to rise in newness[2] of life.

I will come again. I have told you of this experience only to help. I would not have done so unless you were able to apprehend it. It will be meaningless to the seekers of wonders and signs.

You must let self utterly melt away in order that Christ may come to His own.

[1] I Cor. xiii. 8.   [2] Rom. vi. 4.

NINTH LESSON

HE GAVE HIMSELF

A S you unfold in the consciousness of God, many inexplicable things become clear. One is the purifying process of pain. It is safer and grander to suffer, because, rightly viewed, it is sure to perfect the soul. Have you not sometimes felt the shallowness and the emptiness of joy? I tell you it is impossible to know true joy—the heights of joy—until you have known corresponding depths of pain. This is the process called "the refiner's fire."[1] It is cleansing; it is good, and not evil. True joy—the joy of Heaven—should saturate the whole being, and touch the inner consciousness with a sense of its eternity, its everlastingness; and the

[1] Mal. iii. 2.

suffering[1] has prepared a place that joy may enter in. Learn the wisdom in these words: "As sorrowful, yet[2] always rejoicing."

Now I would show you the difference between necessary suffering and useless pain, which is disorder; likewise between true joy and transient false joy. Divine humanity can attain the throne of the universe only by the way of the Cross. This is the way of sacrifice. Do not too hurriedly dismiss the pearl in the old orthodox teaching, it served its day and generation most efficiently. When man thought of himself as a separate and outside unit, only this teaching could help his unfoldment, so thank God for the ladder of dead creeds —dead selves. But now the divine Man is arising; He has burst the old[3] bottles; the new wine of life cries out for space and freedom, as the sap does in the tree. Beware, for here is your danger; the suffering begins, which shall make the path by cleansing and

[1] Isa. ix. 2, 3.   [2] 2 Cor. vi. 10.   [3] Matt. ix. 17.

burning up all that hinders the uprising of the divine in earth, air, and sea. The Son of God is come, and your very experiences of pain and suffering are the heralds of His approach.

There is much more to be revealed to you, but we leave these messages with you to help you to live and express the highest within you, knowing that Christ will perfect that which concerneth Him, and ye are Christ's, and Christ is God's.

INDEX